rainbow knits

rainbow knits

20 colorful knitting patterns in stripes, ombré shades, and variegated yarns

Nicki Trench

CICO BOOKS
LONDON NEW YORK

Published in 2018 by CICO Books
An imprint of Ryland Peters & Small Ltd
20–21 Jockey's Fields, London WC1R 4BW
341 E 116th St, New York, NY 10029
www.rylandpeters.com

10 9 8 7 6 5 4 3 2 1

A CIP catalog record for this book is
available from the Library of Congress and
the British Library.

ISBN: 978 1 78249 564 2

Printed in China

Editor: Marie Clayton
Pattern checker: Jane Czaja
Designer: Alison Fenton
Photographer: Caroline Arber
Stylist: Isabel de Cordova
Illustrator: Stephen Dew

Art director: Sally Powell
Head of production: Patricia Harrington
Publishing manager: Penny Craig
Publisher: Cindy Richards

contents

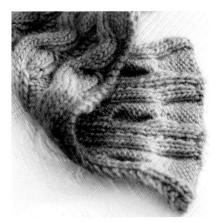

introduction

Bright, colorful rainbow stripes are the ultimate thing to cheer you up. I didn't think I would enjoy myself quite so much as I did when I was designing and making the projects for this book—you can't help but have your spirits lifted by the lovely colors!

There is something for everyone, from garments to gifts, and we also have some beautiful items for the home. There are two blankets that I think you'll really love, one with little geometric squares and the other in gorgeous bold stripes. Both are baby-blanket size, but it's easy to size them up or down. We also have a very on-trend pillow cover in chunky soft cables with bright little rainbow tassels around the edges, and even a funky silk tie and handy little purse if you'd like to make a smaller project.

When knitting with lots of colors you can sometimes have lots of wool left over, so there are many projects to choose from where you can use up leftover yarn. The gorgeously soft Classic Bobble Hat (page 17) uses the same yarn as the Arm Warmers (page 70, one of my favorite projects in the book), and the Silk Tie (page 68) uses the same yarn as the Super Silk Cowl (page 26). For the Embroidered Purse (page 72). you can also use yarn left over from other projects.

There are lots of things to wear: the fabulous Rainbow-striped Cardigan (page 10) or the Striped Turtleneck Sweater (page 22). You'll also find the Cowl really hard to resist and then you'll want to accessorize with the Fair Isle Bag (page 65). So much to choose from!

I've concentrated on using some fun rainbow colors rather than more technical stitching, so there are lots of easy stitches used in this book and if you have any technical difficulties there is a comprehensive Techniques section (pages 74–93) to guide you through. The projects have been knitted on a combination of straight, circular, or double-pointed needles—I tend to use wooden knitting needles as I find they are more forgiving than the metal ones, but use the needles you're used to and feel most comfortable with. You'll find a list of Suppliers at the back of the book that I recommend, and also who supplied many of the materials for the projects in the book.

Sometimes colors and yarns get discontinued, or maybe you can't get hold of them where you live. Don't be afraid to replace yarns with another color or yarn of similar thickness—there's a gauge (tension) guide on nearly all of the projects to help.

I really hope you get to make many of the projects in this book and wear, give, or display your knitted rainbows with pride.

chapter 1
to wear

A really bright, cheerful, and unusual cardigan, with stripes and blocks of color. It's definitely an eye-catcher!

rainbow-striped cardigan

Yarn

Debbie Bliss Baby Cashmerino (55% merino wool, 33% microfiber, 12% cashmere) sportweight (lightweight DK) yarn, approx. 137yd (125m) per 1¾oz (50g) ball

  2:**2**:3:**3**:3:**3** balls of shade 83 Butter (bright yellow) (A)

  2:**2**:2:**3**:3:**3** balls of shade 03 Mint (pale green) (B)

  3:**4**:4:**4**:4:**5** balls of shade 101 Ecru (off-white) (C)

  1:**1**:1:**1**:1:**1** ball each of shades:
  001 Primrose (pale yellow) (D)
  92 Orange (E)
  34 Red (F)
  06 Candy Pink (deep pink) (G)
  87 Damson (purple) (H)

Needles and equipment

US size 2/3 (3mm) and US size 3 (3.25mm) knitting needles

Yarn holder

Yarn sewing needle

8 buttons, ⅝in. (15mm) diameter

Gauge (tension)

25 sts x 34 rows over 4in. (10cm) square, working st st using US size 3 (3.25mm) needles.

Finished size						
To fit size US/UK:	4/8	**6/10**	8/12	**10/14**	12/16	**14/18**
To fit bust:	32	**34**	36	**38**	40	**42in.**
	81	**86**	91	**97**	102	**107cm**
Actual bust:	34	**36**	37¾	**40¼**	42¼	**44in.**
	86.5	**91**	96	**102.5**	107	**112cm**
Length to shoulder:	19¼	**19½**	20	**20¼**	20½	**20¾in.**
	49	**50**	50.5	**51.5**	52	**52.5cm**
Sleeve length:	18	**18½**	18½	**18¾**	18¾	**19½in.**
	46	**47**	47	**48**	48	**49.5cm**

Abbreviations

alt	alternate
approx.	approximate
beg	beginning
cont	continue
dec	decrease
foll	following
inc	increase
k	knit
p	purl
patt	pattern
rem	remain(ing)
rep	repeat
rib 2tog	rib 2 stitches together
RS	right side
st(s)	stitch(es)
st st	stockinette (stocking) stitch
WS	wrong side
yrn	yarn round needle
[]	repeat stitches in brackets number of times stated

for the cardigan

Back

Using US size 2/3 (3mm) needles and A, cast on 110:**116**:122:**130**:136:**142** sts.

Rib row 1: [K1, p1] to end.
Rep last row 13 more times, ending on a WS row.
Change to US size 3 (3.25mm) needles and cont in st st starting with a k row.
Work a further 10 rows.
Dec 1 st at each end of next and foll two 10th rows.
(104:**110**:116:**124**:130:**136** sts)
Cont in patt for 13:**11**:11:**11**:9:**9** rows.

Inc 1 st at each end of next and foll two 10th rows. (110: **116**:122:**130**:136: **142** sts)

Cont in patt until work measures 11¾:**11¾**:11½:**11¼**:11¼:**10½**in. (30:**30**:29:**28.5**:28.5:**27**cm), ending with a WS row.

Shape armholes

Bind (cast) off 5:**5**:6:**6**:6:**7** sts at beg of next 2 rows keeping patt correct. (100:**106**:110:**118**:124:**128** sts)

Cont in A for 2:**2**:4:**4**:6:**6** rows, then fasten off A and join in B, AND AT THE SAME TIME dec 1 st at each end of next 3:**3**:3:**3**:5:**5** rows and then 2:**3**:2:**4**:4:**3** foll RS rows. (90:**94**:100:**104**:106:**112** sts)

Work straight until work measures 19¼:**19½**:19¾:**20¼**:20½:**20¾**in. (49:**50**:50.5:**51.5**:52:**52.5**cm) from cast-on edge, ending with a WS row.

Shape shoulders

Bind (cast) off 10:**11**:12:**12**:12:**13** sts at beg of next 2 rows and 11:**11**:12:**13**:13:**14** sts on foll 2 rows. Leave rem 48:**50**:52:**54**:56:**58** sts on a holder.

Left front

Using US size 2/3 (3mm) needles and C, cast on 52:**55**:58:**62**:65:**68** sts.

Rib row 1: [K1, p1] to end.

Rep last row 5 more times, ending on a WS row.

Change to D and cont in rib for 8 more rows ending on a WS row.

Change to US size 3 (3.25mm) needles, cont in st st working stripe patt as follows:

12 rows in C.
8 rows in E.
10 rows in C.
6 rows in E.
8 rows in B.
4 rows in C.
8 rows in A.
10 rows in C.
8 rows in F.
4 rows in E.
8 rows in C.
8 rows in D.
4 rows in C.
2 rows in G.
2 rows in H.
2 rows in G.
2 rows in H.
2 rows in G.
2 rows in H.
2 rows in G.
2 rows in H.
2 rows in G.
2 rows in H.
8 rows in C.
6 rows in B.
8 rows in F.
10 rows in C.
Work remaining rows in A

Cont straight in stripes until 10 stripe patt rows have been worked. Dec 1 st at beg of next and foll two 10th rows. (49:**52**:55:**59**:62:**65** sts)

Cont in patt for 13:**11**:11:**11**:9:**9** rows. Inc 1 st at beg of next and foll two 10th rows. (52:**55**:58:**62**:65:**68** sts) Cont in patt until work measures same as Back to armhole shaping, ending with a WS row. 11¾:**11¾**:11½:**11¼**:11¼:**10½**in. (30:**30**:29:**28.5**:28.5:**27**cm).

Shape armhole
Bind (cast) off 5:**5**:6:**6**:6:**7** sts at beg of next row keeping stripe patt correct. (47:**50**:52:**56**:59:**61** sts) Work 1 row.
Dec 1 st at armhole edge of next 3:**3**:3:**3**:5:**5** rows then 2:**3**:2:**4**:4:**3** foll RS rows. (42:**44**:47:**49**:50:**53** sts) Work straight until work measures 15:**15¼**:15½:**15¾**:15¾:**15¾**in. (38:**39**:39.5:**40**:40:**40**cm) from cast-on edge, ending with a WS row.

Shape neck
Next row: K to last 8:**9**:9:**10**:10:**10** sts, turn, leaving rem sts on a holder.
Dec 1 st at neck edge on every row until 21:**22**:24:**25**:25:**27** sts rem. Work straight until work measures same as Back to shoulder shaping, ending at armhole edge.

Shape shoulder:
Bind (cast) off 10:**11**:12:**12**:12:**13** sts at beg of next row.
Work 1 row.
Bind (cast) off rem 11:**11**:12:**13**:13: **14** sts.

Right front
Using US size 2/3 (3mm) needles and C, cast on 52:**55**:58:**62**:65:**68** sts.
Rib row 1: [K1, p1] to end.
Cont as for Left Front reversing all shaping.

Sleeve 1
Using US size 2/3 (3mm) needles and D, cast on 54:**58**:62:**62**:66:**70** sts.
Rib row 1: [K1, p1] to end.
Rep last row once more, ending on a WS row.
Change to C.
Rep Row 1 twelve more times, ending on a WS row.
Change to US size 3 (3.25mm) needles and cont in st st with a K row, working the stripe sequence as follows throughout:
18:**18**:18:**20**:22:**22** rows in C.
12 rows in D.
68:**70**:72:**74**:74:**76** rows in C.
2 rows in G.
2 rows in H.
2 rows in G.
2 rows in H.
2 rows in G.
2 rows in H.
2 rows in G.
2 rows in H.
2 rows in G.
2 rows in H.
2 rows in G.
2 rows in H.
Work remaining rows in B.

AT THE SAME TIME shape sleeve as follows:

Work a further 6 rows straight.

Inc 1 st at each end of next and every 6th row to 80:**84**:88:**94**:106:**114** sts.

Cont in stripes until work measures 18¼:**18½**:18½:**18¾**:18¾:**19½**in. (46:**47**:47:**48**:48:**49.5**cm) from cast-on edge, ending with a WS row.

Shape sleeve cap

Bind (cast) off 5:**6**:6:**6**:7:**7** sts at beg of next 2 rows keeping patt correct. (70:**72**:76:**82**:92:**100** sts)

Dec 1 st at each end of next and foll 16:**17**:19:**21**:15:**15** alt rows. (36:**36**:36:**38**:60:**68** sts)

Dec 1 st at each end of every row to 30:**30**:30:**32**:42:**42** sts.

Bind (cast) off 5:**5**:5:**5**:7:**7** sts at beg of next 4 rows.

Bind (cast) off rem 10:**10**:10:**12**:14:**14** sts.

Sleeve 2

Work as for sleeve one replacing D with E.

Button band

With RS facing, using US size 3 (3.25mm) needles and A, pick up and k 97:**99**:101:**103**:103:**103** sts along Left Front edge.

Row 1: P1, [k1, p1] to end.

Row 2: K1, [p1, k1] to end.

Rep last 2 rows twice more.

Bind (cast) off in rib.

Buttonhole band

With RS facing, using US size 2/3 (3mm) needles and A, pick up and k 97:**99**:101:**103**:103:**103** sts along Right Front edge.

Row 1: P1, [k1, p1] to end.

Row 2: K1, [p1, k1] to end.

Work one more row in rib.

Buttonhole row: Rib 3 sts, yrn, rib 2tog, [rib 13:**13**:13:**13**:13:**13** sts, yrn, rib 2tog, rib 12:**13**:13:**13**:13:**13** sts, yrn, rib 2tog] 3 times, rib 5:**4**:6:**8**:8: **8** sts.

Rib 2 rows.

Bind (cast) off in rib.

Neckband

Join shoulder seams.

With RS facing, using US size 2/3 (3mm) needles and A, pick up and k 4 sts from edge of Buttonhole Band, k 8:**9**:9:**10**:10:**10** sts from Right Front neck holder, pick up and k 27:**27**:27:**29**:31:**31** sts up Right Front neck, k 48:**50**:52:**54**:56:**58** sts from Back neck holder, pick up and k 27:**27**:27:**29**:31:**31** sts down Left Front neck, k 8:**9**:9:**10**:10:**10** sts from Left Front holder, pick up and k 5 sts from edge of Button Band. (127:**131**:133:**141**:147:**149** sts)

Row 1: P1, [k1, p1] to end.

Row 2: K1, [p1, k1] to end.

Row 3: P1, [k1, p1] to last 4 sts, yrn, rib 2tog, rib to end.

Row 4: K1, [p1, k1] to end.

Bind (cast) off in rib.

making up and finishing

Sew in ends. Join side and Sleeve seams, sew in Sleeves.

Sew on buttons.

This simple scarf is made using a variegated yarn in gorgeous pinks, so it's self-striping—meaning there are not so many ends to sew in. This is a really interesting pattern and easy to work.

ombré diagonal scarf

Yarn
Louisa Harding Amitola (80% wool, 20% silk) fingering (4ply) yarn, approx. 273yd (250m) per 1¾oz (50g) ball
  2 balls of shade 129 Purple Rain (pink/purple/red)

Needles and equipment
US size 7 (4.5mm) knitting needles

Yarn sewing needle

Gauge (tension)
18 sts x 34 rows over 4in. (10cm) square, working garter st using US size 7 (4.5mm) needles.

Finished size
Length approximately 2¼yd (2m)

Abbreviations
approx.	approximately
k	knit
kfb	knit into the front and back of the next stitch
k2tog	knit two stitches together
patt	pattern
rep	repeat
st(s)	stitch(es)
yo	yarn over (forward)
*	repeat instructions between asterisks

for the scarf
Work in garter st throughout.
Cast on 4 sts.
Row 1: K1, kfb, k to end.
Row 2: K1, k2tog, kfb, k1.

Pattern 1
Row 1: K1, kfb, k to 3 sts before end, k2tog, k1.
Row 2: K to last 2 sts, kfb, k1.
Rep Patt 1 until there are 25 sts.

Pattern 2
Row 1: K1, kfb, *k2tog, yo, k3; rep from * to last 3 sts, k2tog, k1.
Row 2: K to last 2 sts, kfb, k1.
Row 3: K1, kfb, *k2tog, yo, k3; rep from * to last 4 sts, k1, k2tog, k1.
Row 4: Rep Row 2.
Row 5: K1, kfb, *k2tog, yo, k3; rep from * to last 5 sts, k2, k2tog, k1.
Row 6: Rep Row 2.
Work Patt 1 until there are 50 sts.
Work Patt 2 for 6 rows ending with Row 2.

Work Patt 1 until there are 75 sts.
Work Patt 2 for 6 rows.
Work Patt 1 until there are 100 sts.
Work Patt 2 for 6 rows.
Work Patt 1 until there are 125 sts.
Work Patt 2 for 6 rows.
Work Patt 1 until there are 150 sts.
Work Patt 2 for 6 rows.
Bind (cast) off loosely.

making up and finishing

Sew in ends and block to size.

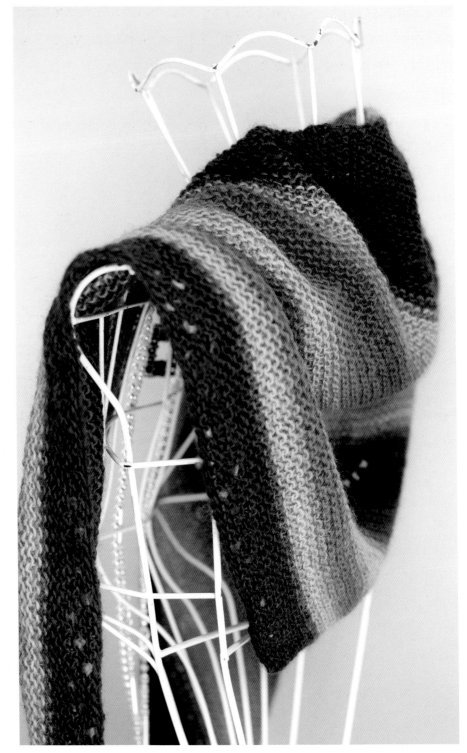

You can't beat a classic bobble hat, and this pattern uses a beautiful rainbow combination of colors in a 100 per cent pure alpaca yarn. This yarn is also used in the arm warmers on page 70.

classic bobble hat

Yarn
Debbie Bliss Aymara (100% alpaca) light worsted (DK) yarn, approx. 109yd (100m) per 1¾oz (50g) hank

  1 hank each of shades:
  10 Copper (orange) (A)
  09 Gold (yellow) (B)
  15 Sky (pale blue) (C)
  16 Storm (dark blue) (D)
  11 Quartz (pink) (E)
  12 Ruby (red) (F)
  14 Moonstone (lilac) (G)
  13 Amethyst (purple) (H)
  08 Moss (olive green) (I)

Needles and equipment
US size 6 (4mm) circular needle, 16in. (40cm) length

US size 6 (4mm) double-pointed needles.

Stitch marker to indicate beginning of round

3 contrast color stitch markers to indicate decreases

Gauge (tension)
Approx. 23 sts x 28 rows over 4in. (10cm) square, working st st using US size 6 (4mm) needles.

Finished size
To fit an average-sized women's head
Approx. 16in. (40.5cm) circumference (unstretched), 12in. (30cm) deep (before turning up cuff)

Abbreviations

alt	alternate
approx.	approximately
beg	begin
cont	continue
dec	decrease(d)
inc	including
k	knit
p	purl
rep	repeat
st(s)	stitch(es)
st st	stockinette (stocking) stitch
k2tog	knit 2 stitches together
ssk	slip 2 stitches knitwise one at a time, knit together through back loops
WS	wrong side
*	repeat instructions between asterisks

Notes

Use the jogless stripes method (see page 88) when joining new colors.

Work 1in. (2.5cm) for each stripe, using the color sequence A, B, C, D, E, F, G, H, I, A, B, C throughout.

Move the marker on each round to denote the start of the round.

for the hat

Brim

Using US size 6 (4mm) circular needle and A, cast on 88 sts.
Place stitch marker and join round, taking care not to twist sts.
Round 1: *K2, p2, (rib): rep from * to end.
Rep round 1 for 4in (10cm), using color sequence.

Main hat

Cont to use color sequence, beg working stripes in st st until work measures approx. 9½in. (24cm) from cast-on edge.

Crown

Beg dec for approx. 3in. (7.5cm). When sts become difficult to work on circular needle, change to double-pointed needles. Keep using same st marker to denote beg of round and as 4th dec point.
Round 1: [K1, ssk, k17, k2tog, place contrast marker] 3 times, k1, ssk, k17, k2tog. (80 sts + 4 st markers placed, with first marker denoting beg of round and first dec point)
Round 2: K to end.
Round 3: [K1, ssk, k to 2 sts before st marker, k2tog, slip marker] 4 times. (72 sts, 8 sts dec)
Rep Rounds 2 and 3 until 16 sts remain.
Last round: K2tog around. (8 sts)

Cut yarn, leaving long tail. Thread tail onto a yarn sewing needle, weave in and out of 8 sts and pull tight, take tail to WS and sew in ends.

making up and finishing

Sew in rest of ends on WS of hat.

Make a pompom (see page 91) with all the yarn colors and attach to the top of the hat.

This scarf is made using a self-patterning yarn, which automatically works up in subtle rainbow stripes. The yarn is chunky and I've used a large, soft cable stitch, which is an eight-stitch cable crossed on every tenth row.

soft cable scarf

Yarn
Louisa Harding Amitola Grande (80% wool, 20% silk) worsted (Aran) yarn, approx. 273yd (250m) per 3½oz (100g) ball
2 balls of shade 519 Embrace (blue/pink/lilac/orange)

Needles and equipment
US size 10 (6mm) knitting needles

Cable needle or double-pointed needle

Row counter

Yarn sewing needle

Gauge (tension)
2 cables (unstretched) x 22 rows over 4in. (10cm) square, working cable patt using US size 10 (6mm) needles.

Finished size
Approx. 60 x 6in. (152 x 15cm)

Abbreviations
approx.	approximately
k	knit
p	purl
patt	pattern
rep	repeat
sl	slip
st(s)	stitch(es)
*	repeat instructions between asterisks

Notes
Use a row counter to mark the 20-row pattern, crossing the cable on Rows 4 and 14.

for the scarf
Cast on 42 sts.
Row 1: K2, *[k2, p8, k2], k1; rep from * twice, k1.
Row 2: K2, *[p2, k8, p2], k1; rep from * twice, k1.
Row 3: Rep Row 1.
Row 4: K2, *[p2, sl next 4 sts onto cable needle and hold in back, k4, k4 from cable needle, p2], k1; rep from * twice, k1.

Rows 5–12: Rep Rows 1 and 2 four times.
Row 13: Rep Row 1.
Row 14: K2, *[p2, sl next 4 sts onto cable needle and hold in front, k4, k4 from cable needle, p2], k1; rep from * twice, k1.
Rows 15–20: Rep Rows 1 and 2 three times.
Rep Rows 1 to 20 until Scarf measures approx. 60in. (152cm) or longer if preferred.
Bind (cast) off.

making up and finishing
Sew in ends and block to size.

This color combination is big favorite of mine. It was fun choosing the random colors and it was a real delight to knit—even better wearing it!

striped turtleneck sweater

Yarn

Debbie Bliss Rialto DK (100% extra-fine merino) light worsted (DK) yarn, approx. 114yd (105m) per 1¾oz (50g) ball

4:**4**:4:**5**:5:**5** balls of shade 04 Grey (A)

2:**2**:2:**2**:2:**2** balls each of shades:

69 Citrus (yellow) (B)

101 Ink (deep blue) (C)

88 Apricot (orange) (D)

76 Rose (pink) (H)

1:**1**:1:**1**:1:**1** ball each of shades:

02 Chocolat (brown) (E)

70 Pool (bright blue) (F)

12 Scarlet (red) (I)

1:**1**:1:**2**:2:**2** balls of shade 02 Ecru (off-white) (G)

Needles and equipment

US size 5 (3.75mm) and US size 6 (4mm) knitting needles

US size 5 (3.75mm) circular needle

Gauge (tension)

27 sts x 30 rows over 4in. (10cm) square, working st st on US size 6 (4mm) needles.

Abbreviations

alt	alternate
approx.	approximate
beg	beginning
cont	continue
dec	decreas(e)ing
foll	follow(ing)
inc	increase
k	knit
p	purl
patt	pattern
rem	remain(ing)
patt	pattern
rep	repeat
st(s)	stitch(es)
st st	stockinette (stocking) stitch
WS	wrong side
*	repeat instructions between asterisks
[ ]	repeat stitches in brackets number of times stated

Back

Stripe sequence for back

12 rows in A.

6 rows in B.

10 rows in C.

2 rows in D.

4 rows in E.

4 rows in F.

6 rows in G.

8 rows in H.

4 rows in A.

8 rows in E.

2 rows in I.

12 rows in A.

2 rows in F.

8 rows in C.

6 rows in I.

10 rows in D.

12 rows in B.

4 rows in H.

10 rows in A.

2 rows in E.

4 rows in F.

2 rows in C.

8 rows in G.

4 rows in B.

4 rows in H.

6 rows in I.

2 rows in C.

6 rows in D.

Work remaining rows in A.

Finished size

To fit size US/UK:	4/8	**6/10**	8/12	**10/14**	12/16	**14/18**
To fit bust:	32	**34**	36	**38**	40	**42in.**
	81	**86**	91	**97**	102	**107cm**
Actual bust:	35	**37¼**	39¼	**41½**	43¾	**46¾in.**
	89	**94.5**	100	**105.5**	111	**116.5cm**
Length:	23¼	**23¾**	24	**24**	24½	**24½in.**
	59	**60**	61	**61**	62	**62cm**

for the sweater

Using US size 5 (3.75mm)
needles and A, cast on
100:**106**:112:**118**:124:**130** sts.
Start stripe sequence, keeping
correct throughout patt.
Row 1: K2, [p2, k2] to end.
Row 2: P2, [k2, p2] to end.
Cont in rib until work measures
2½in. (6cm) ending with a WS row.
Change to US size 6 (4mm) needles,
work st st beg with a k row and
cont working stripe sequence
throughout.
Dec at each end of
11th:**11th**:9th:**9th**:9th:**9th**
row and foll two 12th rows.
(94:**100**:106:**112**:118:**124** sts)

Work a further 15:**15**:15:**13**:13:**13**
rows straight.
Inc at each end of next
row and foll two 12th rows.
(100:**106**:112:**118**:124:**130** sts)
Cont until work measures
15¾:**15¾**:15½:**15¼**:15¼:**14¾**in.
(40:**40**:39.5:**39**:39:**37.5**cm) from cast-
on edge, finishing with a WS row.
Shape armhole
Bind (cast) off 3:**4**:5:**5**:6:**7**
sts at beg of next two rows.
(94:**98**:104:**108**:110:**116** sts)
Dec 1 st at each end of next
and foll 2:**3**:3:**5**:6:**7** alt rows
(88:**90**:94:**96**:98:**100** sts)
**Cont in patt until armhole
measures 7½:**7¾**:8½:**8¾**:9:**9¾**in.
(19:**20**:21.5:**22**:23:**24.5**cm) from beg
of shaping ending with a WS row.
Shape shoulders
Next row: Bind (cast) off
8:**8**:8:**8**:8:**9** sts at beg of next row,
k17:**17**:18:**19**:19:**19**, turn.
Next row: Dec 1, p to end.
(16:**16**:17:**18**:18:**18** sts)
Next row: Bind (cast) off 8:**8**:8:**8**:8:**9**
sts, k to end. (8:**8**:9:**10**:10:**9** sts)
Next row: Dec 1, p to end.
(8:**7**:8:**9**:9:**8** sts)
Bind (cast) off rem 7:**7**:8:**9**:9:**8** sts.
Keeping stripe sequence correct,
rejoin yarn to rem sts with RS facing
and bind (cast) off 38:**40**:42:**42**:44:**44**
sts, k to end.
Complete left shoulder to match
right, reversing shaping.

Front

Work as back until **.
Cont in stripe patt until armhole
measures 3½:**4**:4¼:**4¼**:4½:**5**in.
(9:**10**:11:**11**:11.5:**12.5**cm) from beg
of shaping ending with a WS row.
(88:**90**:94:**96**:98:**100** sts)
Start neck shaping
Next row: K35:**36**:38:**39**:39:**40**, bind
(cast) off 16:**18**:18:**18**:20:**20** sts, patt
to end.
Dec 1 st at neck edge on next and
foll 4 rows, and then on each alt row
to 23:**23**:24:**25**:25:**26** sts.
Cont straight until armhole matches
back to shoulder shaping finishing
on a RS row.
Shape shoulders
Next row: Bind (cast) off 8:**8**:8:**8**:8:**9**
sts, p to end. (15:**15**:16:**16**:16:**18** sts)
Next row: K.
Next row: Bind (cast) off 8:**8**:8:**8**:8:**9**
sts, p to end.
Next row: K.
Bind (cast) off rem 7:**7**:8:**9**:9:**8** sts.
With WS facing, rejoin yarn to rem
sts, p2tog, p to end.
Complete left shoulder to match
right-hand side, reversing all
shaping.

Sleeve

Sleeve stripe sequence

16 rows in A.

4 rows in F.

6 rows in E.

8 rows in H.

8 rows in A.

6 rows in B.

2 rows in C.

4 rows in D.

8 rows in G.

6 rows in F.

2 rows in I.

4 rows in H.

10 rows in C.

2 rows in G.

4 rows in I.

12 rows in A.

4 rows in F.

8 rows in D.

6 rows in E.

10 rows in B.

4 rows in G.

8 rows in H.

Work remaining rows in A.

Using US size 5 (3.75mm) needles and A, cast on 46:**50**:50:**54**:54:**58** sts. Start stripe sequence and cont throughout sleeve.

Row 1: K2, [p2, k2] to end.

Row 2: P2, [k2, p2] to end.

Cont in rib until work measures 2½in. (6cm), ending with a WS row. Change to US size 6 (4mm) needles, work st st beg with a k row and cont working stripe sequence throughout.

Inc 1 at each end of 5th row and every foll 4th row to 52:**56**:62:**60**:66:**66** sts, and then every 6th row to 80:**84**:88:**90**:94:**96** sts. Work straight until sleeve measures 17¾:**17¾**:18:**18**:18½:**18½**in. (45:**45**:46:**46**:47:**47**cm) from cast-on edge.

Shape sleeve cap

Bind (cast) off 3:**4**:5:**5**:6:**7** sts at beg of next two rows. (74:**76**:78:**80**:82:**82** sts) Dec 1 st at each end of next and foll 6:**7**:11:**11**:14:**17** alt rows. (60:**60**:54:**56**:52:**46** sts) Dec 1 st at each end of foll 5:**3**:3:**3**:1:**0** rows. (50:**54**:48:**50**:50:**46** sts)

Bind (cast) off 4:**4**:3:**3**:3:**3** sts at beg of next 6 rows, then bind (cast) off rem 26:**30**:30:**32**:32:**28** sts.

Neckband

Join both shoulder seams.

With RS facing using US size 5 (3.75mm) circular needle, pick up and k 22:**24**:25:**27**:27:**27** sts down left front neck, 16:**18**:18:**18**:20:**20** sts from center front, 22:**24**:25:**27**:27:**27** sts up right front neck, 5 sts from right back side, 38:**40**:42:**42**:44:**44** sts from center back, and 5 sts from left back side. (108:**116**:120:**124**:128: **128** sts)

Join to work in the round.

Next round: [K2, p2] to end.

Cont in rib until neckband measures 2in. (5cm).

Starting with a k row, work 2 rows in st st.

Change to H and work 11 more rows in st st.

Bind (cast) off.

making up and finishing

Join side and Sleeve seams, sew in Sleeves. Sew in ends.

This is a real luxury item. The yarn is a silk mix and the colors are stunning. It's made using a fingering (4-ply) yarn, which means it hangs around the neck beautifully.

super silk cowl

Yarn
Fyberspates Scrumptious 4-ply Sport (55% merino wool, 45% silk) sportweight (4-ply) yarn, approx. 399yd (365m) per 3½oz (100g) hank

1 hank each of shades:
329 Amethyst (purple) (A)
315 Magenta (bright pink) (B)
306 Baby Pink (pale pink) (C)
324 Persimmon (orange) (D)
325 Daffodil (yellow) (E)
311 Flying Saucer (green) (F)
319 Azure (turquoise) (G)
322 Sea Mist (pale blue) (H)

Needles and equipment
US size 6 (4mm) circular needle, 24in. (60cm) long

Stitch marker

Yarn sewing needle

Gauge (tension)
22sts x 42 rows over 4in. (10cm) square, working garter st using US size 6 (4mm) needle.

Finished size
13in. (33cm) deep x 56in. (140cm) around

Note
As this stripe pattern is knitted in the round, use the jogless stripes techniques (see page 88) to keep the ends of the rounds aligned.

Abbreviations
approx. approximately
beg beginning
k knit
p purl
st(s) stitch(es)
st st stockinette (stocking) stitch

for the cowl
Using A, cast on 308 sts. Join into a round very carefully, making sure you don't twist sts. Place stitch marker to denote beg of round. Work in st st throughout (k on RS throughout).
Rounds 1–10: Work in st st (k 1 row, p 1 row).
Fasten off A, join in B.
Using B, work in st st for next 10 rounds.
Fasten off B, join in C.
Using C, work in st st for next 10 rounds.

Fasten off C, join in D.
Using D, work in st st for next 10 rounds.
Fasten off D, join in E.
Using E, work in st st for next 10 rounds.
Fasten off E, join in F.
Using F, work in st st for next 10 rounds.
Fasten off F, join in G.
Using G, work in st st for next 10 rounds.
Fasten off G, join in H.
Using H, work in st st for next 10 rounds.
Continue in this color sequence until cowl measures approx. 13in. (33cm), ending with Round 10.

making up and finishing
Sew in ends.

Block and lightly press edges with a damp cloth.

This tank top is a gorgeous item and it's definitely on trend. It's not only fashionable but also warm, and the colors are beautiful together.

lady's tank top

Yarn

Debbie Bliss Rialto DK (100% extra-fine merino) light worsted (DK) yarn, approx. 114yd (105m) per 1¾oz (50g) ball

5:**5**:5:**6**:6:**7** balls of shade 82 Mallard (blue/green) (MC)

1:**1**:1:**2**:2:**2** balls each of shades:

12 Scarlet (red) (A)

76 Rose (pink) (B)

19 Duck Egg (pale blue) (C)

88 Apricot (orange) (D)

69 Citrus (yellow) (E)

66 Vintage Pink (pale pink) (F)

Needles and equipment

US size 3 (3.25mm) and US size 6 (4mm) knitting needles

Safety pin

Stitch holder

Yarn sewing needle

Gauge (tension)

22 sts x 30 rows over 4in. (10cm) square, working st st using US size 6 (4mm) needles.

Finished size						
To fit size US/UK:	4/8	**6/10**	8/12	**10/14**	12/16	**14/18**
To fit bust:	32	**34**	36	**38**	40	**42in.**
	81	**86**	91	**97**	102	**107cm**
Bust measurement:	34	**36**	38¼	**40½**	42½	**44in.**
	86.5	**92**	97.5	**103**	108	**112cm**
Length:	20	**20½**	20¾	**21¼**	21½	**22in.**
	51	**52**	53	**54**	55	**56cm**

Abbreviations

alt	alternate	**patt**	pattern
approx.	approximately	**PM**	place marker
beg	beginning	**rem**	remaining
cont	continue	**rep**	repeat
dec	decreas(e)ing	**RS**	right side
foll	following	**SM**	slip marker
inc	increase(ing)	**ssk**	slip, slip, knit
k	knit	**st(s)**	stitch(es)
k2tog	knit 2 stitches together	**st st**	stockinette (stocking) stitch
M1	make 1 stitch by picking up and working the loop between 2 stitches	**WS**	wrong side
p	purl	*****	repeat instructions between asterisks

Note

Strand colors not in use loosely on WS of work.

for the tank top

Front

Using US size 3 (3.25 mm) needles and A, cast on 81:**87**:93:**99**:105:**109** sts.

Rib row 1 (RS): K1, *p1, k1; rep from * to end.

Rib row 2 (WS): P1, *k1, p1; rep from * to end.

Change to MC, rep these 2 rows for 2in. (5cm) ending on RS row.

Next row (WS): Rib 3:**6**:1:**4**:7:**2** sts, M1, *rib 5:**5**:6:**6**:6:**7** sts, M1; rep from * to last 3:**6**:2:**5**:8:**2** sts, rib to end. (97:**103**:109:**115**:121:**125** sts)

Change to US size 6 (4mm) needles. Starting with a k row, work in st st until work measures 6: **6½**: 6½: **6½**:6¾:**6½**in.(15.5:**16.5**:16.5:**16.5**:17.5: **16.5**cm) ending on a WS row.

Change to B, work 8 rows in st st.
Change to C, work 8 rows in st st.
Change to D, work 8 rows in st st.

Change to E, work 8 rows in st st.
Change to F, work 8 rows in st st.
Change to MC, work 4 rows in st st.

Shape armholes

Bind (cast) off 4:**5**:5:**6**:7:**7** sts at beg of next 2 rows. (89:**93**:99:**103**:109: **111** sts)

Dec 1 st at each end of next 3:**3**:3:**5**:7:**5** rows, then on foll 5:**5**:5:**4**:3:**4** RS rows. (73:**77**:83:**85**:89:**93** sts)

P 1 row.***

Divide for neck:

Next row (RS): Dec 1 st, patt until there are 35:**37**:40:**41**:43:**45** sts on right-hand needle, turn and complete this side first.

Work 1 row.

Sizes US 8–12/UK 12–18 only

Dec 1 st at armhole edge, work to last 2 sts before neck edge, k2tog, on every RS row to –:–:37:**36**:36:**42** sts. Keeping armhole straight cont to dec 1 st at neck edge on every alt row until 22:**23**:25:**26**:25:**32** sts rem, then on every 4th row until 17:**19**:20:**20**:20:**24** sts rem.

Work straight until armhole measures 8³/₈:**8³/₈**:8³/₄:**9**:9:**9³/₄**in:. (21:**21**:22:**23**:23:**25**cm) from start, ending with WS row.

Shape shoulder

Bind (cast) off 6:**7**:7:**7**:7:**8** sts at beg of next and foll alt row.

Work 1 row.

Bind (cast) off rem 5:**5**:6:**6**:6:**8** sts.

With RS facing, slip center st onto a safety pin. Rejoin yarn to rem sts and k to last 2 sts, k2tog. (35:**37**:40:**41**:43:**45** sts)

Complete to match first side of neck, reversing shapings.

Back

Work as for Front to ***.

Dec on each end of next and every foll alt row to 71:**75**:79:**79**:81:**89** sts. Cont straight in st st until armhole matches Front to shoulder shaping.

Shape shoulders

Bind (cast) off 6:**7**:7:**7**:7:**8** sts at beg of next 4 rows, then 5:**5**:6:**6**:6:**8** sts on next 2 rows.

Cut yarn, and leave rem 37:**37**:39:**39**:41:**41** sts on st holder.

Neck border

Join right shoulder seam with back stitch.

With RS facing and using US size 3 (3.25 mm) needles and MC, pick up and k 37:**37**:39:**42**:42:**46** sts down left front neck, PM, k1 from safety pin, pick up and k 37:**37**:39:**42**:42:**46** sts up right front neck, then k across 37:**37**:39:**39**:41:**41** sts from st holder, inc 1 st at center back. (112:**112**:118:**124**:126:**134** sts)

Row 1 (WS): *P1, k1; rep from * until 1 st before marker, p1, SM, **k1, p1; rep from ** to end.

Row 2 (RS): *K1, p1; rep from * until 3 sts before marker, p1, ssk, SM, k1, k2tog, **p1, k1; rep from ** to end.

Row 3 (WS): *P1, k1; rep from * until 4 sts before marker, p1, k2tog, p1, SM, ssk, p1, **k1, p1; rep from ** to end.

Rep last 2 rows once more.

Change to A and work Rows 2–3 once more.

Bind (cast) off in rib, dec on each side of center st as set.

Armhole borders

Join left shoulder and neck border seam with backstitch.

With RS facing and using US size 3 (3.25 mm) needles and MC, pick up and k 95:**95**:99:**103**:103:**111** sts evenly around armhole edge.

Beg with Rib Row 2, work in rib as given for Front for 5 rows.

Change to A and work 2 more rows in rib.

Bind (cast) off in rib.

making up and finishing

Sew in ends and block to size.

Join side seams using backstitch.

chapter 2
babies *and* children

This cute little cardigan, with its pretty, bright rainbow stripes across the yoke, will brighten up any baby's day.

rainbow-yoke baby cardigan

Yarn
Debbie Bliss Baby Cashmerino (55% merino wool, 33% microfiber, 12% cashmere) sportweight (lightweight DK) yarn, approx. 137yd (125m) per 1¾oz (50g) ball
  3 balls of shade 101 Ecru (off-white) (MC)
  ⅛ ball each of shades:
  34 Red (A)
  78 Lipstick Pink (pink) (B)
  91 Acid Yellow (yellow) (C)
  02 Apple (green) (D)
  71 Pool (blue) (E)

Needles and equipment
US size 2 (2.75mm) and US size 3 (3.25mm) knitting needles

US size 2 (2.75mm) and US size 3 (3.25mm) circular needles

2 stitch holders

Yarn sewing needle

6 small buttons

Gauge (tension)
25 sts x 34 rows over 4in. (10cm) square, working st st using US size 3 (3.25mm) needles.

Finished size
To fit ages: 3–6:**6–9**:9–12 months
Chest measurement:
19¾:**22**:24½in. (50:**56**:62cm)
Length to shoulder:
8¾:**9½**:10¼in. (22:**24**:26cm)
Sleeve length:
5½:**6¼**:7in. (14:**16**:18cm)

Abbreviations
alt	alternate
beg	beginning
cont	continue
dec	decrease
foll	following
inc	increase
k	knit
k2tog	knit 2 stitches together
p	purl
rem	remain(ing)
rep	repeat
rib 2tog	work 2 stitches together keeping rib pattern correct
RS	right side
st(s)	stitch(es)
st st	stockinette (stocking) stitch
WS	wrong side
yo	yarn over (forward)
*	repeat instructions between asterisks

Notes
The first row of picking up the stitches for the yoke is knitted in the main color (MC).

The stripes on the yoke are five rows of each color.

for the cardigan

(make 1)

Using US size 2 (2.75mm) needles and MC, cast on 125:**141**:157 sts.

Rib row 1: P1, *k1, p1; rep from * to end.

Rib row 2: K1, *p1, k1; rep from * to end.

Rep the last 2 rows 2:**2**:3 times more. Change to US size 3 (3.25mm) needles. Beg with a k row, work in st st until work measures 4¾:**5**:5½in. (12:**13**:14cm) from cast-on edge, ending with a WS row.

Divide for Back and Fronts

Next row: K31:**35**:39 sts, leave these sts on a holder for Right Front, k next 63:**71**:79 sts and leave these sts on a holder for Back, k to end.

Left front

Work straight on last set of 31:**35**:39 sts for 2:**4**:6 rows, ending with a k row.

Shape yoke

Bind (cast) off 6 sts at beg (front edge) of next row, 3 sts at beg of 3 foll alt rows, then 2 sts on 3:**4**:5 foll alt rows. Now dec 1 st at beg of every foll alt row until 3:**5**:7 sts rem.

Cont straight until Left Front measures 8¾:**9½**:10¼in. (22:**24**:26cm) from cast on-edge, ending at armhole edge.

Shape shoulder

Bind (cast) off.

Back

With WS facing, rejoin yarn to next st on back holder, p63:**71**:79 sts. Work straight on these sts for 2:**4**:6 rows.

Shape yoke

Next row: K25:**29**:33 sts, turn and work on these sts.

Bind (cast) off 3 sts at beg of next row, and 2 foll alt rows, then 2 sts on 3:**4**:5 foll alt rows.

Now dec 1 st at beg of every foll alt row until 3:**5**:7 sts rem.

Cont straight until back measures 8¾:**9½**:10¼in. (22:**24**:26cm) from cast-on edge, ending at armhole edge.

Shape shoulder

Bind (cast) off.

With RS facing, slip center 13 sts onto a holder, rejoin yarn to rem 25:**29**:33 sts, k to end.

Next row: P.

Complete to match first side of Back.

Right front

With WS facing, rejoin yarn to next st on Right Front, p to end.

Work straight on these 31:**35**:39 sts for 2:**4**:6 rows.

Shape yoke

Cast off 6 sts at beg of next row, 3 sts at beg of 3 foll alt rows, then 2 sts on 3:**4**:5 foll alt rows.

Now dec 1 st at beg of every foll alt row until 3:**5**:7 sts rem.

Cont straight until front measures 8¾:**9½**:10¼in. (22:**24**:26cm) from cast-on edge, ending at armhole edge.

Shape shoulder

Bind (cast) off.

Yoke

Join shoulder seams using mattress stitch. With RS facing and using US size 3 (3.25mm) circular needle and MC, pick up and k 40:**44**:48 sts on Right Front neck edge, 35:**39**:43 sts on Right Back neck edge, k across 13 sts from stitch holder, pick up and k 35:**39**:43 sts on Left Back neck edge and 40:**44**:48 sts on Left Front neck edge. (163:**179**:195 sts)

Change to A.

Beg with a p row, work 3 rows st st.

Dec row: K5, k2tog, *k6, k2tog; rep from * to last 4 sts, k4. (143:**157**:171 sts)

Next row: P.

Change to B.

Dec row: Using B, k4, k2tog, *k5, k2tog; rep from * to last 4 sts, k4. (123:**135**:147 sts)

Work 4 rows in st st, starting with a p row.

Change to C.

Next row: P.

Work 4 more rows in st st in C.

Change to D.

Dec row: K3, *k2tog, k5, k2tog, k3; rep from * to end. (103:**113**:123 sts)

Work 4 rows in st st in D.

Change to E.

Next row: P.

Dec row: K3 *k2tog, k3; rep from * to end. (83:**91**:99 sts)

Next row: P.

Dec row: K3, *k2tog, k2; rep from * to end. (63:**69**:75 sts)

Next row: P.

Change to US size 2 (2.75mm) circular needle and MC.

Rib row 1: K1, *p1, k1; rep from * to end.

Rib row 2: P1, *k1, p1; rep from * to end.

Rep last two rows once more.

Bind (cast) off.

Button band

With RS facing and using US size 2 (2.75mm) needles and MC, pick up and k 55:**61**:67 sts along Left Front edge.

Work 4 rows rib as given for Back and Fronts.

Bind (cast) off in rib.

Buttonhole band

With RS facing and using US size 2 (2.75mm) needles and MC, pick up and k 55:**61**:67 sts along Right Front edge.

Work 1 row rib as given for Back and Fronts.

Buttonhole row: Rib 2, [rib 2tog, yo, rib 8:**9**:10 sts] 5 times, rib 2tog, yo, rib 1:**2**:3 sts. Rib 2 rows.

Bind (cast) off in rib.

Sleeves

(make 2)

Using US size 2 (2.75mm) needles and MC, cast on 36:**40**:44 sts.

Work 6:**8**:10 rows in [k1, p1] rib.

Change to US size 3 (3.25mm) needles.

Do not break yarn, carry MC up side of stripes.

Beg with a k row, work in st st, inc 1 st at each end of 3rd and every foll 4th row until there are 54:**58**:62 sts.

Work first 2 rows in A, break yarn, work next 2 rows in B, break yarn, cont rem sleeve in MC.

Cont straight until sleeve measures 5½:**6¼**:7in. (14:**16**:18cm) from cast-on edge, ending with a p row.

Bind (cast) off.

making up and finishing

Sew in ends. Join the Sleeve seams using mattress stitch. Sew the Sleeves into the armholes using mattress stitch.

Sew on buttons to match the buttonhole positions.

This blanket pattern combines a lovely soft off-white with striking stripes. It's made in garter stitch, so is a really good project for a beginner knitter.

baby blanket

Yarn

Debbie Bliss Rialto DK (100% extra-fine merino) light worsted (DK) yarn, approx. 114yd (105m) per 1¾oz (50g) ball

9 balls of shade 02 Ecru (off-white) (MC)

2 balls each of shades:

12 Scarlet (red) (A)

69 Citrus (yellow) (B)

71 Jade (green) (C)

72 Ocean (dark blue) (D)

76 Rose (pink) (E)

Needles and equipment

US size 6 (4mm) circular needle, 40in. (100cm) long

Yarn sewing needle

Gauge (tension)

20 sts x 40 rows over 4in. (10cm) square, working garter st using US size 6 (4mm) needles.

Finished size

Approx. 30 x 37in. (76 x 94cm)

Abbreviations

alt	alternate
approx.	approximately
cont	continue
k	knit
inc	knit in front and back of next st
rep	repeat
st(s)	stitch(es)

Notes

Use a circular needle but knit in straight rows, turning at the end of each row.

Work in garter stitch (every row knit) throughout.

for the blanket

Using MC, cast on 152 sts.

K 44 rows (approx. 4in./10cm).

K 14 rows (approx. 1½in./4cm) in each color sequence as follows: A, MC, B, MC, C, MC, D, MC, E. Cont in MC for 66 rows (approx. 6in./15cm).

K 14 rows (approx. 1½in./4cm) in each color sequence as follows: E, MC, D, MC, C, MC, B, MC, A. Change to MC.

K 44 rows (approx. 4in./10cm). Bind (cast) off.

Edging

Short ends

With RS facing and using A, starting at one corner, pick up and k 150 sts along one short end.

Row 1: Inc in first st, k to end, inc in last st. (152 sts)

Change to B.

Row 2: Rep Row 1. (154 sts)

Change to C.

Rows 3 and 4: Rep Row 1. (156 sts)

Change to E.

Rows 5 and 6: Rep Row 1. (158 sts)

Change to MC.

Row 7: K to end.

Bind (cast) off.

Rep on other short end.

Long sides

With RS facing and using A, starting at one corner, pick and k 200 sts along one long side.

Rep Rows 1 to 7 of short ends.

Rep on other long side.

making up and finishing

Sew corners of Edging together, matching stripes.

Sew in ends and block to size.

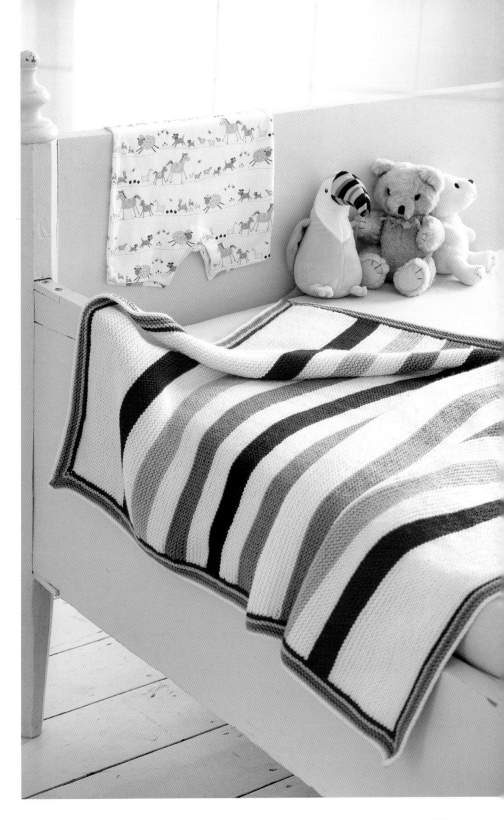

toy rabbit

A cute and fat rainbow rabbit is fit for any age group! This one is made using a very lovely soft yarn that has a small percentage of cashmere. Stuff it lightly so that it's super squidgy and cuddly.

Yarn

Debbie Bliss Baby Cashmerino (55% merino wool, 33% microfiber, 12% cashmere) sportweight (lightweight DK) yarn, approx. 137yd (125m) per 1¾oz (50g) ball

1 ball each of shades:
101 Ecru (off-white) (MC)
02 Apple (green) (A)
91 Acid Yellow (yellow) (B)
204 Baby Blue (blue) (C)
78 Lipstick Pink (pink) (D)
34 Red (E)

Small amount each of black and pale pink for features

Needles and equipment

US size 3 (3.25mm) knitting needles

Yarn sewing needle

Toy stuffing

Gauge (tension)

Gauge (tension) is not critical on this project, size is approximate according to gauge.

Finished size

Approx. length from tip to toe: 11½in. (29cm)

Abbreviations

approx.	approximately
beg	begin(ning)
cont	continue
k	knit
k2tog	knit 2 stitches together
kfb	knit into the front and back of the next stitch
M1L	make 1 left: pick up strand between the two needles from the front to back with the tip of left needle, knit into the back of this stitch
M1R	make 1 right: pick up strand between the two needles from back to front with the tip of left needle, knit into the front of this stitch
p	purl
p2tog	purl 2 stitches together
p2tog tbl	purl 2 stitches together through the back loops
pfb	purl into the front and back of the next stitch
rem	remaining
rep	repeat
RS	right side
ssk	slip 2 stitches knitwise one at a time, knit together through back loops
st(s)	stitch(es)
st st	stockinette (stocking) stitch
WS	wrong side
[ ]	repeat stitches in brackets number of times stated

for the rabbit

Arms

(make 2)

Using MC, cast on 4 sts.

Row 1 (RS): [Kfb] to end. (8 sts)
Row 2 (WS): P.
Row 3: [Kfb] to end. (16 sts)
Row 4: P.
Row 5: [K3, kfb] to end. (20 sts)
Row 6–8: Beg with a WS p row, work 3 rows in st st.
Row 9: [K3, k2tog] to end. (16 sts)
Rows 10–20: Beg with a WS p row, work 11 rows in st st.
Row 21: [K6, k2tog] to end. (14 sts)
Rows 22–24: Beg with a WS p row, work 3 rows in st st.
Row 25: K2tog, k10, ssk. (12 sts)
Row 26: P4, p2tog, p2tog tbl, p4. (10 sts)
Row 27: K2tog, k6, ssk. (8 sts)
Row 28: P2, p2tog, p2tog tbl, p2. (6 sts)
Row 29: K2tog, k2, ssk. (4 sts)
Row 30: P2tog, p2tog tbl. (2 sts)
Row 31: K2tog.

Cut yarn, leaving long tail for sewing up later, thread end through rem sts to fasten off.

Legs

(make 2)

Using MC, cast on 4 sts.

Row 1 (RS): [Kfb] to end. (8 sts)

Row 2 (WS): [Pfb] to end. (16 sts)

Row 3: K.

Row 4: [P3, pfb] to end. (20 sts)

Row 5: [K4, kfb] to end. (24 sts)

Rows 6–10: Beg with a WS p row, work 5 rows in st st.

Row 11: [K4, k2tog] to end. (20 sts)

Row 12: [P3, p2tog] to end. (16 sts)

Rows 13–24: Beg with a RS k row, work 12 rows in st st.

Cut yarn leaving an 8in. (20cm) tail, place sts on holder and put to one side for later.

Rep Rows 1–24 for second leg, but keep sts on needle at end of Row 24. Do not bind (cast) off but cont for Body. Cut MC, leaving an approx. 3in. (7.5cm) tail.

Body

Row 1 (RS): Join A, k16 of second leg, k across the 16 sts held on a st holder from the first leg. (32 sts)

Row 2 (WS): P.

Row 3: K1, M1L, k2, M1R, k2, M1L, k7, M1R, k8, M1L, k7, M1R, k2, M1L, k2, M1R, k1. (40 sts)

Row 4: P.

Cut A leaving an approx. 3in. (7.5cm) tail.

Row 5: Join B, k2, M1L, k2, M1R, k4, M1L, k7, M1R, k10, M1L, k7, M1R, k4, M1L, k2, M1R, k2. (48 sts)

Row 6: P.

Row 7: K3, M1L, k2, M1R, k6, M1L, k7, M1R, k12, M1L, k7, M1R, k6, M1L, k2, M1R, k3. (56 sts)

Row 8: P.

Cut B leaving an approx. 3in. (7.5cm) tail.

Row 9: Join C, k4, M1L, k2, M1R, k8, M1L, k7, M1R, k14, M1L, k7, M1R, k8, M1L, k2, M1R, k4. (64 sts)

Rows 10–12: Beg with a WS p row, work 3 rows in st st.

Cut C, leaving an approx. 3in. (7.5cm) tail.

Rows 13–16: Join D, work 4 rows in st st.

Cut D, leaving an approx. 3in. (7.5cm) tail.

Rows 17–20: Join E, work 4 rows in st st.

Cut E, leaving an approx. 3in. (7.5cm) tail.

Rows 21–24: Join MC, work 4 rows in st st.

Row 25: Cont with MC, p3, p2tog tbl, p2, p2tog, p6, p2tog tbl, p30, p2tog, p6, p2tog tbl, p2, p2tog, p3. (58 sts)

Shape chest and shoulder

Row 1 (RS): K.

Row 2 (WS): P.

Row 3: K2, k2tog, k2, ssk, k4, k2tog, k30, ssk, k4, k2tog, k2, ssk, k2. (52 sts)

Row 4: P.

Row 5: K.

Row 6: P1, p2tog tbl, p2, p2tog, p2, p2tog tbl, p7, p2tog, p12, p2tog tbl, p7, p2tog, p2, p2tog tbl, p2, p2tog, p1. (44 sts)

Row 7: K.

Row 8: P.

Row 9: K5, k2tog, k8, ssk, k10, k2tog, k8, ssk, k5. (40 sts)

Row 10: P.

Row 11: K3, k2tog, k10, ssk, k6, k2tog, k10, ssk, k3. (36 sts)

Row 12: P.

Row 13: K15, ssk, k2, k2tog, k15. (34 sts)

Row 14: P.

Shape head

Rows 1–19: Using MC, beg with a RS k row, work 19 rows in st st.

Row 20 (WS): P8, p2tog tbl, p14, p2tog, p8. (32 sts)

Row 21 (RS): [K2tog] to end. (16 sts)

Row 22: P.

Row 23: [K2tog] to end. (8 sts)

Row 24: [P2tog] to end. (4 sts)

Cut yarn, leaving long tail for sewing up later, thread end through 4 rem sts to fasten off.

Ears

(make 2)

Using MC, cast on 4 sts.

Row 1: [Kfb] to end. (8 sts)

Row 2: P.

Row 3: [Kfb] to end. (16 sts)

Beg with WS p row, work 5 rows st st.

Row 9: *K3, k2tog; rep from * to last st, k1. (13 sts)

Beg with WS p row, work 7 rows st st.

Row 17: *K4, k2tog; rep from * to last st, k1. (11 sts)

Row 18: *P2, p2tog, rep to last 3 sts, p last 3 sts. (9 sts)

Bind (cast) off.

making up and finishing

Oversew the Arm seams, stuffing before finishing the seam. Sew the Arms onto the Body.

Oversew the Leg seams and stuff lightly. Continue up to sew the seam of the Body and Head, stuffing fairly firmly as you go.

Using mattress stitch, sew the Ear seams on the RS, and sew the Ears to the top of the Head.

Embroider French knots (see page 92) for the eyes with a scrap of black yarn. Work a triangle in satin stitch for the nose in pale pink yarn. Embroider the mouth in D, using straight stitches (see page 92.)

The dots on this hat are made using Swiss darning, and they really stand out against the dark gray to make a bright and fun child's hat. If you don't want the dots, the basic pattern is great for beginners.

child's pompom hat

Yarn

Hat

Debbie Bliss Falkland Aran (100% wool) worsted (Aran) yarn, approx. 196yd (180m) per 3½oz (100g) hank

   1 hank of shade 03 Charcoal (gray) (MC)

Dots and pompoms

Mrs Moon Plump DK (80% superfine merino, 20% baby alpaca) light worsted (DK) yarn, approx. 125yd (115m) per 1¾oz (50g) hank

   Small amount each of shades:
   Lemon Curd (yellow)
   Marmalade (orange)
   Raspberry Ripple (deep pink)
   Bonbon (blue)
   Pistachio Ice Cream (green)

Needles and equipment

US size 8 (5mm) knitting needles

Yarn sewing needle

2in. (5cm) pompom maker, or pair of 2in. (5cm) cardstock rings

Gauge (tension)

19 stitches x 26 rows over 4in. (10cm) square, working st st using a US size 8 (5mm) knitting needle.

Finished size

Approx. 8½in. (22cm) wide, 6in. (15cm) deep

Abbreviations

approx.	approximately
cont	continue
k	knit
rep	repeat
st(s)	stitch(es)
st st	stockinette (stocking) stitch
WS	wrong side
*****	repeat instructions between asterisks

for the hat

(make 2 sides the same)

Using MC, cast on 40 sts.

Rows 1–4: *K2, p2 (rib): rep from * to end.

Row 5: K to end.

Row 6: P to end.

Cont in st st as set, until work measures approx. 6in. (15cm). Bind (cast) off.

making up and finishing

With WS together, sew the side and top seams.

adding dots

Work Swiss darning (see page 92) over the top of stitches approx. 2 sts apart and 2 rows apart, alternating colors. Thread a yarn sewing needle with a tail of yarn in the chosen color. Bring the point of the needle through from the back at the base of the stitch to be worked onto, and

draw the yarn through, leaving an end at the back. Take the needle behind the two loops of the stitch directly above from right to left. Draw the yarn through. Insert the needle back into the base of the stitch being worked onto, and pull the yarn through to the back again.

Cut the yarn and secure both ends by sewing in on the WS.

Make two pompoms (see page 91) approx. 2in. (5cm) in diameter, using all colors from the dots. Sew the pompoms securely at each top corner of the Hat.

I have had the most fun making this blanket. I loved choosing from these gorgeous shades and putting the colors together. The squares are small, but the pattern is easy—so it might take time to knit all the squares, but the result is definitely worth it.

squares baby blanket

Yarn
Debbie Bliss Baby Cashmerino Tonals (55% wool, 33% acrylic, 12% cashmere) sportweight (lightweight DK) yarn, approx. 137yd (125m) per 1¾oz (50g) ball

3 balls each of shades:
- 13 Citrus (yellow)
- 20 Ruby (red)
- 14 Leaf (green)
- 19 Rose (pink)
- 17 Aqua (bright blue)

5 balls of shade 16 Sky (pale blue)

Needles and equipment
US size 3 (3.25mm) knitting needles

US size 3 (3.25mm) circular needle, 48in. (120cm) long

Yarn needle

Gauge (tension)
Each square measures approx. 2¾in. (7cm) square, using US size 3 (3.25mm) knitting needles.

Finished size
Each square measures 2¾in. (7cm) square
Blanket measures approx. 33 x 44in. (84 x 112cm) including border

Abbreviations
alt	alternate
approx.	approximately
cont	continue
inc	increase
k	knit
k1tbl	knit 1 stitch through the back loop
p	purl
rep	repeat
RS	right side
sl1p	slip 1 stitch purlwise with yarn in front
s2togkpo	with yarn at back, slip 2 stitches together knitwise, knit 1, pass 2 slipped stitches over
st(s)	stitch(es)

Color combinations
Make a total of 198 squares, 33 squares in each colorway

1: A = pale blue; B = yellow
2: A = red; B: = bright blue
3: A = pink; B = green
4: A = yellow; B = pale blue
5: A = bright blue; B = red
6: A = green; B = pink

for the square

Using US size 3 (3.25mm) straight knitting needles and A, cast on 31 sts.

Row 1: K to end.

Row 2: Sl1p, k13, s2togkpo, k13, k1tbl. (29 sts)

Row 3 and all alt rows: Sl1p, k to last st, k1tbl.

Row 4: Sl1p, k12, s2togkpo, k12, k1tbl. (27 sts)

Row 6: Sl1p, k11, s2togkpo, k11, k1tbl. (25 sts)

Row 8: Sl1p, k10, s2togkpo, k10, k1tbl. (23 sts)

Row 9: Sl1p, k to last st, k1tbl.

Cut A, join B.

Row 10: Sl1p, k9, s2togkpo, k9, k1tbl. (21 sts)

Row 11: Cont to rep Row 3 on every foll alt row.

Row 12: Cont in B, sl1p, k8, s2togkpo, k8, k1tbl. (19 sts)

Row 14: Sl1p, k7, s2togkpo, k7, k1tbl. (17 sts)

Row 16: Sl1p, k6, s2togkpo, k6, k1tbl. (15 sts)

Row 18: Sl1p, k5, s2togkpo, k5, k1tbl. (13 sts)

Row 20: Sl1p, k4, s2togkpo, k4, k1tbl. (11 sts)

Row 22: Sl1p, k3, s2togkpo, k3, k1tbl. (9 sts)

Row 24: Sl1p, k2, s2togkpo, k2, k1tbl. (7 sts)

Row 26: Sl1p, k1, s2togkpo, k1, k1tbl. (5 sts)

Row 28: Sl1p, s2togkpo, k1tbl. (3 sts)

Row 30: S2togkpo.

Cut yarn and pull through last stitch to fasten off.

making up and finishing

Lay the squares out RS up on a flat surface with colors randomly placed, with 12 squares across x 16 squares down. With RS together, sew the squares together in strips using whipstitch and one of the colors from each pair of squares, to disguise the stitching.

Press the seams lightly using a damp cloth.

border

Using A and US size 3 (3.25mm) circular needle, and with RS facing, pick up and k 180 sts along top edge. (15 sts along each square)

K 8 rows AND AT THE SAME TIME inc 1 st at each end of all RS rows.

Bind (cast) off.

Pick up and k 180 sts along bottom edge.

K 8 rows AND AT THE SAME TIME inc 1 st at each end of all RS rows.

Bind (cast) off.

Pick up and k 240 sts along one side edge.

K 8 rows AND AT THE SAME TIME inc 1 st at each end of all RS rows.

Bind (cast) off.

Pick up and k 240 sts along second side edge.

K 8 rows AND AT THE SAME TIME inc inc 1 st at each end of all RS rows.

Bind (cast) off.

With RS together, sew border seams at the corners.

A lovely cozy and bright sweater, which knits up really beautifully in this yarn. The stripe is created by using a self-patterning "print" yarn, so as you're knitting it, you never know what colors you're going to get—which is like dipping your fingers into a paint box! And the colors are really effective.

baby sweater

Yarn

Debbie Bliss Rialto DK (100% extra-fine merino) light worsted (DK) yarn, approx. 114yd (105m) per 1¾oz (50g) ball
  3:3:4:4:5 balls of shade 02 Ecru (off-white) (MC)
Debbie Bliss Rialto DK Prints (100% extra-fine merino) light worsted (DK) yarn, approx. 114yd (105m) per 1¾oz (50g) ball
  1:1:2:2:2 balls of shade 14 Seaside (multicolored) (A)

Needles and equipment

US size 4 (3.5mm) knitting needles

Stitch holder

Yarn sewing needle

3 buttons

Gauge (tension)

22 sts x 31 rows over 4in. (10cm) square, working st st using US size 4 (3.5mm) needles.

Finished size

	0–6	6–12	12–18	18–24	24–36
To fit age in months:					
Chest:	20¼	23	24½	25¾	28½in.
	50.5	58.5	62	65.5	72.5cm
Length to shoulder:	9¾	11½	12¾	14	15in.
	24.5	29	32	35.5	38cm
Sleeve length:	5½	6	7½	9	9in.
	14	15	19	23	23cm

Abbreviations

alt	alternate	**RS**	right side
cont	continue	**ssk**	slip 2 stitches knitwise one at a time, knit together through back loops
dec	decrease		
foll	following		
inc	increase(ing)	**st(s)**	stitch(es)
k	knit	**st st**	stockinette (stocking) stitch
p	purl	**WS**	wrong side
patt	pattern	**yon**	yarn over needle
p2tog	purl 2 stitches together	**[ ]**	repeat stitches in brackets number of times stated
rem	remain(ing)		
rib 2tog	work 2 stitches together keeping rib pattern correct	*	repeat instructions between asterisks

for the sweater

Back

Using US size 4 (3.5mm) needles and A, cast on 62:**66**:70:**74**:82 sts.

Rib row 1: K2, *p2, k2; rep from * to end.

Rib row 2: P2, *k2, p2; rep from * to end.

Change to MC and cont in rib for a further 6:**8**:8:**10**:10 rows.

Change to A.

Starting with a k row, work in st st for 20 rows.**

Change to MC.

Work until 44:**56**:64:**72**:82 more rows of st st. (9:**11**:12¼:**13¼**:14½in./ 23:**27.5**:30.5:**33.5**:36.5cm from bottom edge)

Shape shoulders

Next row: K19:**20**:21:**23**:25 sts, turn.

Cont on these sts only, work a further 3 rows in st st.

Bind (cast) off.

Rejoin yarn to rem sts and bind (cast) off 24:**26**:28:**28**:32 sts, k to end.

Next row: P19:**20**:21:**23**:25 sts.

Place rem sts on st holder or scrap of yarn.

Front

Work as Back to **.

Change to MC.

Work a further 36:**48**:54:**62**:72 rows of st st.

Start neck shaping

Next row: K22:**23**:24:**26**:28 sts, bind (cast) off 18:**20**:22:**22**:26 sts, k to end.

Next row: P to end.

Next row: Ssk, k to end.

Next row: P.

Cont to dec 1 st on neck edge on every alt row until 19:**20**:21:**23**:25 sts rem.

Work a further 5:**5**:7:**7**:7 rows.

Bind (cast) off.

With WS facing, rejoin yarn to rem 22:**23**:24:**26**:28 sts, p to end.

Next row: K to end.

Next row: P2tog, p to end.

Cont to dec 1 st at neck edge on every alt row until 19:**20**:21:**23**:25 sts rem.

Work a further 2:**2**:4:**4**:4 rows.

Place rem sts on st holder or scrap of yarn.

Sleeves

(make 2)

Using US size 4 (3.5mm) needles and A, cast on 34:**34**:38:**38**:42 sts.

Rib row 1: K2, *p2, k2; rep from * to end.

Rib row 2: P2, *k2, p2; rep from * to end.

Change to MC and cont in rib for a further 6:**6**:8:**8**:10 rows.

Change to A, work 8 rows in st st starting with a k row, inc 1 st at each end of 3rd row and every foll 6th:**4th**:8th:**8th**:8th row.

Change to MC and cont inc as above to 44:**46**:48:**52**:56 sts.

Cont in st st until a total of 34:**36**:50:**60**:60 st st rows have been worked.

Bind (cast) off.

Neckband

Join right shoulder.

With RS facing and using MC, pick up and k 7:**7**:9:**9**:9 sts down left Front neck, k 18:**20**:22:**22**:26 sts from center Front, pick up and k 10:**10**:12:**12**:12 sts up right Front neck, pick up and k 3 sts from side of Back neck, k 24:**26**:28:**28**:32 sts from center Back, pick up and k 1 st up left Back neck. (63:**67**:75:**75**:82 sts)

Rib row 1: P2, *k2, p2; rep from * to end.

Rib row 2: K2, *p2, k2; rep from * to end.

Change to A.

Work a further 2 rows in rib as set.

Place sts on st holder or scrap yarn.

Back button band

With RS facing and using MC, pick up and k 3:**4**:3:**3**:3 sts along edge of neckband and k 19:**20**:21:**23**:25 sts along left shoulder. (22:**24**:24:**26**:28 sts)

Row 1: P2:**0**:0:**2**:0, [k2, p2] to end.

Row 2: *K2, p2; rep from * to last 2:**0**:0:**2**:0 sts, k2:**0**:0:**2**:0.

Change to A, work a further 4 rows in rib as set.

Bind (cast) off in rib.

Front buttonhole band

With RS facing and using MC, k 19:**20**:21:**23**:25 sts along left shoulder and pick up and k 3:**4**:3:**3**:3 sts along edge of neckband. (22:**24**:24:**26**:28 sts)

Row 1: P2:**0**:0:**2**:0, [k2, p2] to end.

Row 2: *K2, p2; rep from * to last 2:**0**:0:**2**:0 sts, k2:**0**:0:**2**:0.

Next row (WS): Change to A. Rib 2 sts, [yon, rib 2tog, rib 5:**6**:6:**7**:7 sts] twice, yon, rib 2tog, rib 4:**4**:4:**4**:6 sts.

Next row: Rib to end.

Work a further 2 rows in rib.

Bind (cast) off in rib.

Complete neckband

With RS facing and using A, pick up and rib 4 sts along edge of buttonhole band, rib all sts from neckband, pick up and rib 4 sts along edge of button band.

Rib 1 more row.

Bind (cast) off in rib.

making up and finishing

Attach the buttons so the bands overlap and the right-hand side is the same length as the left-hand side and button up left shoulder.

Attach the left sleeve, sewing it to both shoulder bands. Attach the right sleeve. Sew up the side and sleeve seams.

Sew in ends and block to size.

chapter 3
gifts and *home*

This is a beautiful yarn to work with—as the name suggests, it's plump, but delightfully soft. Mittens are a lovely project to make; quick for when the cold weather hits you, they also make really charming gifts.

striped mittens

Yarn
Mrs Moon Plump DK (80% superfine merino, 20% baby alpaca) light worsted (DK) yarn, approx. 125yd (115m) per 1¾oz (50g) hank

 1 hank each of shade:
 Cherry Pie (red) (A)
 Raspberry Ripple (deep pink) (B)
 Marmalade (orange) (C)
 Lemon Curd (yellow) (D)
 Pistachio Ice Cream (green) (E)
 Bonbon (blue) (F)

Needles and equipment
US size 6 (4mm) and US size 8 (5mm) double-pointed needles

Yarn sewing needle

Stitch holder

Stitch marker to indicate beginning of round

2 contrast color stitch markers to indicate space for thumb gusset

Gauge (tension)
16 sts x 26 rows over 4in. (10cm) square, working st st using US size 8 (5mm) needles.

Finished size
To fit an average-sized woman's hand Approx. 10in. (25cm) long x 4in. (10cm) wide

Abbreviations
approx.	approximately
beg	beginning
cont	continu(e)ing
inc	increase
k	knit
k2tog	knit 2 stitches together
p	purl
PM	place marker
rem	remaining
rep	repeat
RS	right side
SM	slip marker
st(s)	stitch(es)
st st	stockinette (stocking) stitch
WS	wrong side
*	repeat instructions between asterisks

Notes
Divide each hank of wool into two equal balls.

Mittens are worked using yarn doubled throughout.

Each mitten is worked in the round using double-pointed needles. Where st st is indicated, each round should be worked in k on RS.

for the mittens

(make 2)

Cuff

Using A double and US size 6 (4mm) double-pointed needles, cast on 36 sts. Divide onto 3 needles and join round, taking care not to twist sts. PM to mark beg of round.

Work K1, p1 rib for 17 rounds, or until work measures approx. 3in. (7.5cm).

Start two-row stripe

Cont using yarn double and work in color order B, C, D, E, F, A throughout. Change to US size 8 (5mm) double-pointed needles and knit in st st for 6 rounds until work measures approx. 4in. (10cm) from beg.

Thumb shaping

Round 1: Cont two-row color striping, k17, inc 1 in next st, k to end. (37 sts)

Round 2: K17, PM (first contrast marker) to mark thumb gusset, k3, PM (second contrast marker) to mark thumb gusset, k to end.

Round 3: K to first contrast marker, SM, inc 1 in each of next 2 sts, k1 (to second contrast marker), SM, k to end. (5 sts between contrast markers)

Round 4: K to end. (5 sts between contrast markers)

Round 5: K to first contrast marker, SM, inc 1 in next st, k to last 2 sts before second contrast marker, inc 1 in next st, k1, SM, k to end. (7 sts between contrast markers)

Round 6: K to end. (7 sts between contrast markers)

Rep Rounds 5 and 6 twice more (11 sts between contrast markers)

Next round: K to first contrast marker, remove marker, k1, slip next 11 sts onto st holder, k1, remove second contrast marker, k to end. Work in st st on rem 36 sts until piece measures approx. 8½in. (21cm) from beg.

Shape top

Round 1: *K4, k2tog; rep from * to end. (30 sts)

Round 2: K to end.

Round 3: *K3, k2tog; rep from * to end. (24 sts)

Round 4: K to end.

Round 5: *K2, k2tog; rep from * to end. (18 sts)

Round 6: K to end.

Round 7: *K1, k2tog; rep from * to end. (12 sts)

Round 8: K to end.

Round 9: K2tog around. (6 sts)

Cut yarn, leaving a long tail. Draw tail through rem stitches using yarn sewing needle. Pull tightly and fasten off.

Thumb

Using US size 8 (5mm) double-pointed needles, divide 11 sts from st holder evenly onto 3 needles. Working on RS, join yarn and pick up and k 3 sts along inside edge of hand, k rem stitches. (14 sts)

PM to indicate beg of round.

Work in st st for 5 rounds or until Thumb measures approx. 2½in. (6.5cm).

Next round: *K2tog to last st, k1. (6 sts)

Cut yarn, leaving a long tail. Draw tail through rem stitches with yarn sewing needle and pull tightly together to secure. Fasten off.

making up and finishing

Sew in ends and block to size.

cable pillow with rainbow tassels

I just love big, chunky knitted pillows. If a colorful rainbow pillow doesn'tfit with your decor, then try this subtler, one-color pillow with rainbow tassels. I used up some scraps of Debbie Bliss Baby Cashmerino for the tassels, but you can use any scraps you have in your stash. If you prefer, you could make a second knitted panel for the other side instead of backing it with fabric.

Yarn

Debbie Bliss Roma (70% wool, 30% alpaca) super bulky (super chunky) yarn, approx. 87yd (80m) per 3½oz (100g) ball

 4 balls of shade 08 Citrus (yellow)
 Scraps of yarn in red, purple, pale pink, teal blue, bright pink, purple, turquoise, pale blue, dark green, orange, candy pink

Needles and equipment

US size 19 (15mm) knitting needles

Large cable needle

Row counter

Yarn sewing needle

20 x 20in. (50 x 50cm) pillow form

Approx. 21 x 21in. (52.5 x 52.5cm) of fabric backing (OR an additional 4 balls of 08 Citrus)

Sewing needle and thread to match fabric

Gauge (tension)

7 sts x 10 rows over 4in. (10cm) square, working cable patt using US size 19 (15mm) needles with yarn doubled.

Finished size

20in. (50cm) square

Abbreviations

approx.	approximately
k	knit
p	purl
rep	repeat
sl	slip
st(s)	stitch(es)
[ ]	repeat stitches in brackets number of times stated

Notes

Use a row counter to mark the 16-row pattern, crossing the cable on Rows 4 and 12.

for the pillow

(make 1)

Using yarn doubled throughout, cast on 36 sts.

Row 1: K13, [k2, p6, k2], k13.
Row 2: K13, [p2, k6, p2], k13.
Row 3: Rep Row 1.
Row 4: K13, [p2, sl next 3 sts onto cable needle and hold in back, k3, then k3 from cable needle, p2], k13.
Rows 5–10: Rep Rows 1 and 2 three times.
Row 11: Rep Row 1.
Row 12: K13, [p2, sl next 3 sts onto cable needle and hold in front, k3, then k3 from cable needle, p2], k13.
Rows 13–16: Rep Rows 1 and 2 twice.
Rep Rows 1–16 until Pillow measures 20in. (50cm).
Bind (cast) off.

making up and finishing

Sew in ends and block to size.

backing

Fold and press a 1in. (2.5cm) hem to the WS on each side of the fabric. With WS together, hand-sew the fabric to the knitted piece around 3 sides. Insert the pillow form, and continue to sew along last side to close.

tassels

Make 44 tassels, using multicolor yarn scraps. Cut the multicolor scraps into 5½in (14cm) lengths. Take 15 strands of one color and fold them in half. With the right side of the cushion facing you, insert a crochet hook through one of the edge stitches from the wrong side. Catch the loop at the fold point of the strands with the hook, and pull it through the stitch. Remove the crochet hook and pull the tails of the strands through the loop. Pull on the strands to tighten the tassel.

Attach the tassels (11 each side), approx. 1½in (4cm) apart along the seams.

I love using a knitted passport cover—it keeps my passport safe and I can store my boarding pass inside it too. This colorful design also makes it really easy to find my passport in my hand luggage when I'm traveling. I have mixed and matched yarns here and used colors I had available.

passport cover

Yarn

Debbie Bliss Rialto DK (100% extra-fine merino) light worsted (DK) yarn, approx. 115yd (105m) per 1¾oz (50g) ball

1 ball each of shades:

02 Ecru (off-white) (MC)

12 Scarlet (red) (A)

44 Aqua (pale blue) (C)

77 Heather (dark pink) (E)

66 Vintage Pink (pale pink) (F)

Mrs Moon Plump DK (80% superfine merino, 20% baby alpaca) light worsted (DK) yarn, approx. 125yd (115m) per 1¾oz (50g) hank

1 hank each of shades:

Pistachio Ice Cream (green) (B)

Marmalade (orange) (D)

Needles and equipment

US size 6 (4mm) knitting needles

Yarn sewing needle

Two pieces of lining fabric, each 6 x 7in. (15 x 18cm)

20in. (50cm) of ribbon, ¾in. (1.5cm) wide

Gauge (tension)

26 stitches x 25 rows over 4in. (10cm) square, working st st using a US size 6 (4mm) knitting needles.

Finished size

Approx. 5 x 6in. (12.5 x 15cm)

Abbreviations

approx.	approximately
beg	begin(ning)
cont	continue
k	knit
rep	repeat
RS	right side
st(s)	stitch(es)
st st	stockinette (stocking) stitch
WS	wrong side
*****	repeat instructions between asterisks

Notes

Seed (moss) st is worked over an odd number of stitches, beginning and ending with K1.

Chart is read right to left on odd-numbered (RS) rows and left to right on even-numbered (WS) rows.

Strand colors not in use loosely on WS of work.

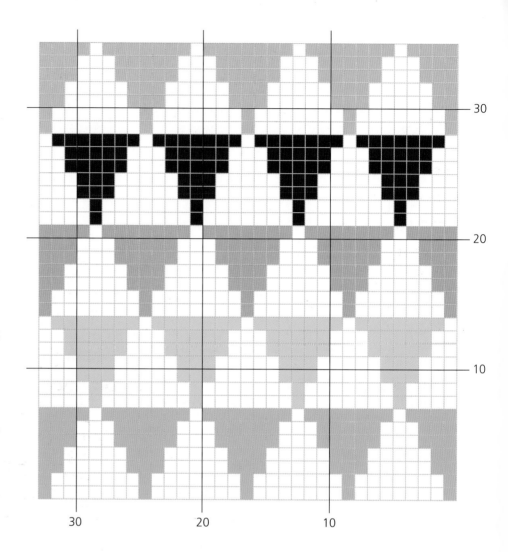

for the cover

(work in one piece)

Using A, cast on 33 sts.

Work in seed (moss) st as follows:

Rows 1–4: K1, *p1, k1 (seed/moss st); rep from * to end.

Cut A.

Working in st st throughout starting with a k row, follow 35 rows of Chart using MC as background color throughout and additional colors as shown.

At end of Chart, k three rows in st st using F (bottom of Passport Cover).

Turn Chart upside down and work again for second side of Passport Cover, now working colors in order F, E, D, C, B.

Change to A, purl to end.

Cont with A, work seed (moss) st for 4 rows.

Bind (cast) off.

making up and finishing

Sew in ends and block to size.

With RS together, fold the Cover in half matching the seed (moss) stitch borders. Pin and then sew the seams with backstitch. Turn the Cover RS out.

lining

Make up the lining (see page 93). Cut the ribbon in half and stitch the end of one length at the top of the Cover between the knitted piece and the lining. Repeat with the other length on the other side. Oversew the top edge of the lining inside the top edge of the knitted piece, securing the ribbon ties at the same time.

These are a great way of keeping extra warm in winter! I'm addicted to arm warmers and especially when made using this gorgeous 100 per cent alpaca yarn, which is supersoft and comes in beautiful colors. The same yarn is also used in the Classic Bobble Hat project on page 17.

arm warmers

Yarn
Debbie Bliss Aymara (100% alpaca) light worsted (DK) yarn, approx. 109yd (100m) per 1¾oz (50g) hank

1 hank each of shades:
13 Amethyst (purple) (A)
14 Moonstone (lilac) (B)
12 Ruby (red) (C)
11 Quartz (pink) (D)
10 Copper (orange) (E)
09 Gold (yellow) (F)
15 Sky (pale blue) (G)
16 Storm (dark blue) (H)
08 Moss (olive green) (I)

Needles and equipment
US size 4 (3.5mm) double-pointed needles

Yarn sewing needle

Gauge (tension)
24 sts x 32 rows over 4in. (10cm) square, working garter st using US size 4 (3.5mm) needles.

Finished size
Approx. length 13½in. (34cm)

Abbreviations
approx.   approximately
k   knit
st(s)   stitches

Note
Use the jogless stripes method (see page 88) when joining new colors.

for the arm warmers
(make 2)
Using A, cast on 40 sts, divide equally over three needles and join into a ring, taking care not to twist sts.
K 14 rows in A.
K 12 rows (approx. 1½in./4cm) in each color, in sequence B, C, D, E, F, G, H.
K 14 rows in I.
Bind (cast) off.

making up and finishing
Sew in ends and block to size.

I love knitted purses and there is a current trend for embroidery that works really well on this purse. It's not only perfect for coins and notes—I also use mine for jewelry and contact lenses when I'm out and about. You can never have enough little purses like this.

embroidered purse

Yarn
Debbie Bliss Rialto DK, 100% extra-fine merino light worsted (DK) yarn, approx. 114yd (105m) per 1¾oz (50g) ball
  1 ball of shade 70 Pool (blue)
  Scraps of red, yellow, orange, pale pink, mid-pink, bright pink, lilac, green, dark blue

Needles and equipment
US size 6 (4mm) knitting needles

Yarn sewing needle

Approx. 7½ x 11in. (19 x 28cm) of fabric lining

Sewing needle and matching thread

6in. (15cm) red closed-end zipper

Gauge (tension)
21 sts x 32 rows over 4in. (10cm) square, working st st using US size 6 (4mm) needles.

Finished size
Approx. 6 x 4in. (15 x 10cm)

Abbreviations
approx.	approximately
beg	beginning
k	knit
p	purl
RS	right side
st st	stockinette (stocking) stitch
st(s)	stitch(es)
WS	wrong side

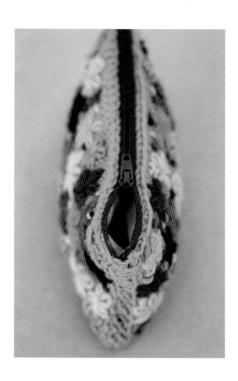

for the purse

Cast on 33 sts.
Beg with a k row, work in st st until work measures approx. 8in. (20cm).
Bind (cast) off.

making up and finishing

Sew in ends. Pin and block piece to size.

Using scraps and the photo on the right as a guide, embroider lazy daisies and French knots (see page 92) on the RS of the Purse.

With RS together, fold the Purse in half so that the cast-on and bound (cast)-off edges meet, then oversew the side seams. Turn RS out.

Make up the lining as described on page 93. With WS facing, sew the zipper into the opening of the lining. Insert the lining into the Purse with WS together, and sew the top edges of the Purse down on either side of the zipper teeth.

techniques

In this section you'll find the basic knitting techniques that you will need for most of the patterns in this book.

The knitting needles, yarn, and other items that you need are listed at the beginning of each of the pattern instructions. You can substitute the yarn recommended in a pattern with the same weight of yarn in a different brand, but you will need to check the gauge (tension). When calculating the quantity of yarn you require, it is the length of yarn in each ball that you need to check, rather than the weight of the ball; the length of yarn per ball in each recommended project yarn is given in the pattern.

Gauge (tension)

A gauge (tension) is given with each pattern to help you make your item the same size as the sample. The gauge is given as the number of stitches and rows you need to work to produce a 4-in (10-cm) square of knitting.

Using the recommended yarn and needles, cast on 8 stitches more than the gauge (tension) instruction asks for—so if you need to have 10 stitches to 4in (10cm), cast on 18 stitches. Working in pattern as instructed, work eight rows more than is needed. Bind (cast) off loosely.

Lay the swatch flat without stretching it. Lay a ruler across the stitches as shown, with the 2in (5cm) mark centered on the knitting, then put a pin in the knitting at the start of

the ruler and at the 4in (10cm) mark: the pins should be well away from the edges of the swatch. Count the number of stitches between the pins. Repeat the process across the rows to count the number of rows to 4in (10cm).

If the number of stitches and rows you've counted is the same as the number asked for in the instructions, you have the correct gauge (tension). If you do not have the same number then you will need to change your gauge (tension).

To change gauge (tension) you need to change the size of your knitting needles. A good rule of thumb to follow is that one difference in needle size will create a difference of one stitch in the gauge

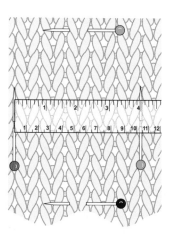

(tension). You will need to use larger needles to achieve fewer stitches and smaller ones to achieve more stitches.

Holding needles

If you are a knitting novice, you will need to discover which is the most comfortable way for you to hold your needles.

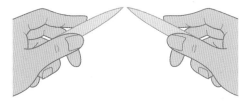

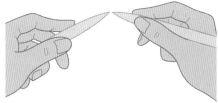

Like a knife
Pick up the needles, one in each hand, as if you were holding a knife and fork—that is to say, with your hands lightly over the top of each needle, 2–3in. (5–7.5cm) from the needle tips.

Like a pen
Now try changing the right hand so you are holding the needle as you would hold a pen, with your thumb and forefinger lightly gripping the needle close to its pointed tip and the shaft resting in the crook of your thumb. As you knit, you will not need to let go of the needle but simply slide your right hand forward to manipulate the yarn.

Holding yarn

As you knit, you will be working stitches off the left needle and onto the right needle, and the yarn you are working with needs to be tensioned and manipulated to produce an even fabric. To hold and tension the yarn you can use either your right or left hand. Try both methods to discover which works best for you.

Yarn in right hand
To knit and purl in the US/UK style (see pages 79 and 80), hold the yarn in your right hand.

To hold the yarn tightly (above left), wind it right around your little finger, under your ring and middle fingers, then pass it over your index finger; this finger will manipulate the yarn.

For a looser hold (above right), catch the yarn between your little and ring fingers, pass it under your middle finger, then over your index finger.

Yarn in left hand
To knit and purl in the Continental style (see pages 79 and 80), hold the yarn in your left hand.

To hold the yarn tightly (above left), wind it right around your little finger, under your ring and middle fingers, then pass it over your index finger; this finger will manipulate the yarn.

For a looser hold (above right), fold your little, ring, and middle fingers over the yarn, and wind it twice around your index finger.

Making a slip knot

You will need to make a slip knot to start knitting; this knot counts as the first cast-on stitch.

1 With the ball of yarn to the right, lay the end of the yarn on the palm of your left hand. With your right hand, wind the yarn twice around your index and middle fingers to make a loop. Make a second loop behind the first one. Slip a knitting needle in front of the first loop to pick up the second loop, as shown.

2 Slip the yarn off your fingers, leaving the loop on the needle. Gently pull on both yarn ends to tighten the knot a little, then pull on the yarn leading to the ball of yarn to fully tighten the knot on the needle.

Casting on (cable method)

There are a few methods of casting on, but the one used for most projects in this book is the cable method, which uses two needles.

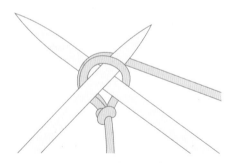

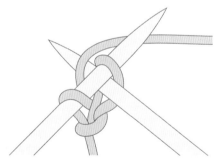

1 Make a slip knot as outlined above. Put the needle with the slip knot into your left hand. Insert the point of your other needle into the front of the slip knot and under the left needle. Wind the yarn from the ball of yarn around the tip of the right needle.

2 Using the tip of your needle, draw the yarn through the slip knot to form a loop. This loop is your new stitch. Slip the loop from the right needle onto the left needle.

3 To make the next stitch, insert the tip of your right needle between the two stitches. Wind the yarn over the right needle, from left to right, then draw the yarn through to form a loop. Transfer this loop to your left needle. Repeat until you have cast on the right number of stitches for your project.

Making a knit stitch—US/UK style

1 Hold the needle with the cast-on stitches in your left hand, and then insert the tip of the right needle into the front of the first stitch, from left to right. Wind the yarn around the point of the right needle, from left to right.

2 With the tip of your right needle, pull the yarn through the stitch to form a loop. This loop is your new stitch.

3 Slip the original stitch off the left needle by gently pulling your right needle to the right. Repeat these steps until you have knitted all the stitches on your left needle. To work the next row, transfer the needle with all the stitches into your left hand.

Making a knit stitch—Continental style

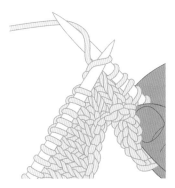

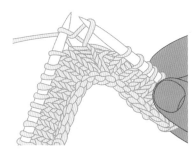

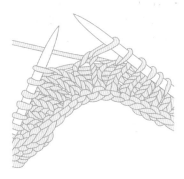

1 Hold the needle with the stitches to be knitted in your left hand, and then insert the tip of the right needle into the front of the first stitch from left to right. Holding the yarn fairly taut with your left hand at the back of your work, use the tip of your right needle to pick up a loop of yarn.

2 With the tip of your right needle, bring the yarn through the original stitch to form a loop. This loop is your new stitch.

3 Slip the original stitch off the left needle by gently pulling your right needle to the right. Repeat these steps until you have knitted all the stitches on your left needle. To work the next row, transfer the needle with all the stitches into your left hand.

Making a purl stitch—US/UK style

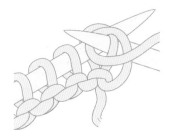  

1 Hold the needle with the stitches in your left hand, and then insert the tip of the right needle into the front of the first stitch, from right to left. Wind the yarn around the point of the right needle, from right to left.

2 With the tip of the right needle, pull the yarn through the stitch to form a loop. This loop is your new stitch.

3 Slip the original stitch off the left needle by gently pulling your right needle to the right. Repeat these steps until you have purled all the stitches on your left needle. To work the next row, transfer the needle with all the stitches into your left hand.

Making a purl stitch—Continental style

 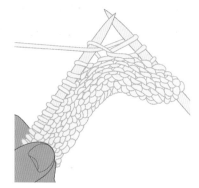 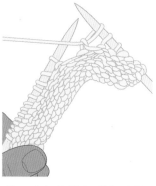

1 Hold the needle with the stitches to be knitted in your left hand, and then insert the tip of the right needle into the front of the first stitch from right to left. Holding the yarn fairly taut at the back of your work, use the tip of your right needle to pick up a loop of yarn.

2 With the tip of your right needle, bring the yarn through the original stitch to form a loop.

3 Slip the original stitch off the left needle by gently pulling your right needle to the right. Repeat these steps until you have purled all the stitches on your left needle. To work the next row, transfer the needle with all the stitches into your left hand.

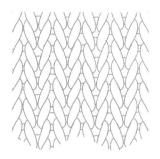

Stockinette (stocking) stitch

This stitch makes a fabric that is different on each side; the knit side is flat and the purl side is textured. To make this stitch, work alternate rows of knit and purl stitches. The front of the fabric is the side on which to work the knit rows.

Garter stitch

This stitch forms a ridged fabric that is the same on both sides. To make this stitch, you simply knit every row.

Ribbing

This stitch has vertical ridges and it creates an elastic fabric with stretch, for cuffs and edges. It is worked by alternating knit and purl stitches, and on the following row purling the knit stitches and knitting the purl stitches. Shown here is a 1x1 stitch rib, but you can work different numbers of stitches for wider ridges.

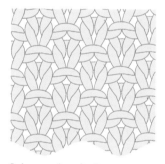

Seed (moss) stitch

To make this stitch, knit and purl alternate stitches across a row. On the next row, knit the knit stitches and purl the purl stitches to create a firm, textured pattern.

Binding (casting) off

In most cases, you will bind (cast) off knitwise, which means that you will knit the stitches before you bind (cast) them off.

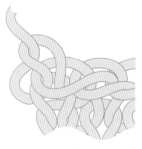

1 First knit two stitches in the normal way. With the point of your left needle, pick up the first stitch you have just knitted and lift it over the second stitch. Knit another stitch so that there are two stitches on your needle again. Repeat the process of lifting the first stitch over the second stitch. Continue this process until there is just one stitch remaining on the right needle.

2 Break the yarn, leaving a tail of yarn long enough to stitch your work together. Pull the tail all the way through the last stitch. Slip the stitch off the needle and pull it fairly tightly to make sure it is secure.

Increasing
A few methods of increasing are used in this book

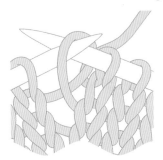

Make 1 (M1)
Pick up the horizontal strand between two stitches with your left-hand needle from front to back. Knit into the back of the loop, transferring the stitch to the right-hand needle in the normal way. It is important to knit into the back of the loop so that the yarn is twisted and does not form a hole in your work. This is also sometimes abbreviated as M1L.

For make 1 right (M1R), pick up the horizontal strand between two stitches with your left-hand needle from back to front. Knit into the front of the loop, transferring the stitch to the right-hand needle in the normal way.

Knit in front and back of next stitch (kfb)

This creates an extra stitch, so it is also sometimes abbreviated as "inc" in a knitting pattern.There will be a visible bar of yarn across the base of the extra stitch.

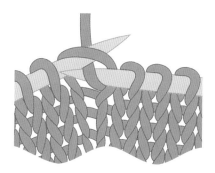

1 Knit the next stitch on the left-hand needle in the usual way, but do not slip the original stitch off the left-hand needle.

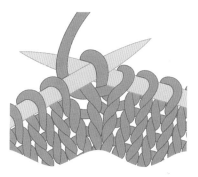

2 Move the right-hand needle behind the left-hand needle and put it into the same stitch again, but through the back of the stitch this time. Knit the stitch through the back loop (see page 84).

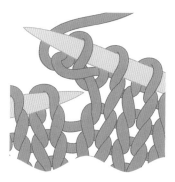

3 Slip the original stitch off the left-hand needle. You have increased by one stitch.

Purl in front and back of next stitch (pfb)

This creates an extra stitch, so is also sometimes abbreviated as "inc" when working a purl row, or "inc purlwise."

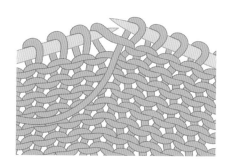

1 Purl the next stitch on the left-hand needle in the usual way, but do not slip the original stitch off the left-hand needle.

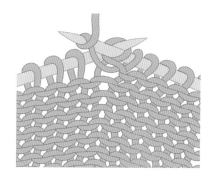

2 Twist the right-hand needle backward to make it easier to put it into the same stitch again, but through the back of the stitch this time. Purl the stitch through the back loop (see page 84).

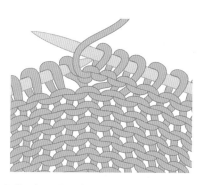

3 Slip the original stitch off the left-hand needle. You have increased by one stitch.

Through the back loop

You usually knit or purl stitches by putting the right-hand needle into the front of the stitch. However, sometimes a stitch needs to be twisted to create an effect or to work a technique, and to do this you knit or purl into the back of it. This is called working "through the back loop" and is abbreviated to "tbl" in a knitting pattern.

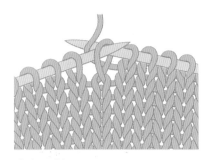

Knitting tbl
Put the right-hand needle into the back of the next stitch on the left-hand needle. Knit the stitch in the usual way, but through the back loop.

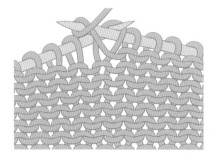

Purling tbl
Put the right-hand needle into the next stitch on the left-hand needle. Purl the stitch in the usual way, but through the back loop.

Yarnovers

Making a yarnover involves winding the yarn around the right-hand needle to make an extra loop that is worked as a stitch on the next row. As well as increasing the stitch count, a yarnover makes a small eyelet.

How a yarnover is made depends on the stitches either side of it; in the US all versions are called "yarnover" and are abbreviated to "yo," but in the UK each method has a separate name and abbreviation.

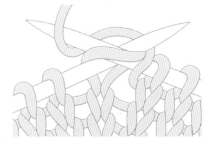

Yarnover between knit stitches
In the UK this is called "yarn forward" and is abbreviated to "yfwd."
1 Bring the yarn between the tips of the needles to the front. Take the yarn over the right-hand needle to the back and knit the next stitch on the left-hand needle.

Yarnover between purl stitches
In the UK this is called "yarn round needle" and is abbreviated to "yrn."
1 Wrap the yarn over and right around the right-hand needle. Purl the next stitch on the left-hand needle.

Yarnover between purl and knit stitches
In the UK this is called "yarn over needle" and is abbreviated to "yon."
1 Leaving the yarn at the front of the work, put the needle knitwise into the next stitch on the left-hand needle. Take the yarn over the right-hand needle to the back and knit the stitch.

Decreasing

There are several ways of decreasing.

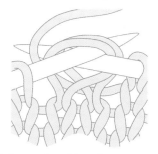

Knit 2 together (k2tog)
This is the simplest way of decreasing. Simply insert your needle through two stitches instead of the normal one when you begin your stitch and then knit them in the normal way.

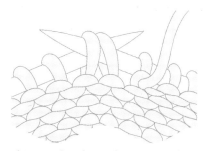

Purl 2 together (p2tog)
Simply insert your needle through two stitches instead of one when you begin your stitch and then purl them in the normal way.

Purl 2 stitches together through the back loops (p2tog tbl)
Starting at the back of the work, insert the right needle into the back of the next two stitches, from left to right. This will feel counter-intuitive but it is correct; the needle will emerge toward the front. Then purl the two stitches together from this position.

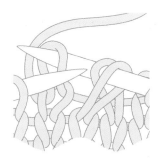

Slip 2 stitches together knitwise, knit 1, pass slipped st over (s2togkpo)
With yarn at back, slip two stitches together knitwise, knit the next stitch, then pass the two slipped stitches over.

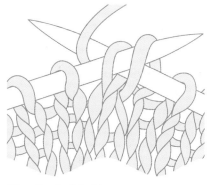

Slip, slip, knit (ssk)
Slip one stitch and then the next stitch knitwise onto your right-hand needle, without knitting them. Then insert the left-hand needle from left to right through the front loops of both the slipped stitches and knit them together.

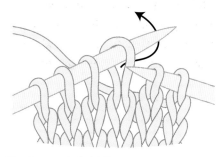

Slipping a stitch (sl1)
Sometimes you will need to transfer a stitch from the right needle to the left needle without knitting it, which is known as slipping a stitch. Simply insert your right-hand needle into the stitch in the normal way, as if you were going to knit or purl it. Then instead of knitting the stitch, pull your right-hand needle further to the right so that the stitch "falls" off the left-hand needle and is transferred to the right-hand needle. The illustration shows a stitch being slipped knitwise.

Cables

Cables involve moving groups of stitches, and you will need a cable needle to hold the stitches being moved. Work a six-stitch cable as shown here: if it is a four stitch cable, then slip two stitches onto the needle and knit two, rather than three. For an eight-stitch cable, slip four stitches onto the needle and knit four.

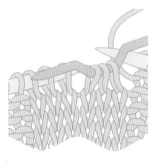

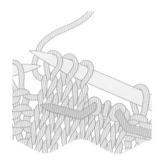

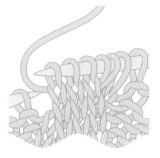

Working a six-stitch front cable

1 Work to the position of the cable. Slip the next three stitches on the left-hand needle onto the cable needle, keeping the cable needle in front of the work. Leave the three stitches on the cable needle in the middle so they don't slip off.

2 Knit the next three stitches off the left-hand needle in the usual way.

3 Then knit the three stitches off the cable needle and the cable is completed.

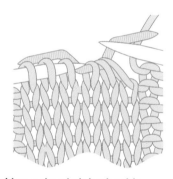

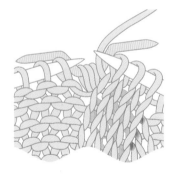

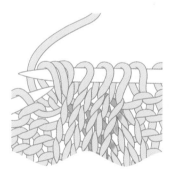

Working a six-stitch back cable

1 Work to the position of the cable. Slip the next three stitches on the left-hand needle onto the cable needle, keeping the cable needle at the back of the work. Leave the three stitches in the middle of the cable needle so they don't slip off.

2 Knit the next three stitches off the left-hand needle in the usual way.

3 Then knit the three stitches off the cable needle and the cable is completed.

Making pompoms

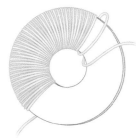

Cardboard rings method

1 Using a pair of card rings cut to the size pompom you would like to create, cut a length of yarn and wind it around the rings until the hole in the center is filled.

2 Cut through the loops around the outer edge of the rings and ease them slightly apart. Thread a length of yarn between the layers and tie tightly, leaving a long end. Remove the card rings and fluff up the pompom. The long yarn tail can be used to sew the pompom in place.

Book method

Use this method to make larger pompoms.

1 Leaving a long tail, wrap the yarn around a paperback book (or something a similar size) about 120 times, leaving a second long tail.

2 Ease the wrapped yarn off the book gently and wrap the second tail tightly around the center six or seven times.

3 Take a yarn sewing needle and thread in the second tail. Push the needle through the center wrap backward and forward three or four times.

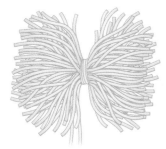

4 Cut the loops on each side of the wrap. Holding the two tails in one hand, hold the bobble and fluff it out.

5 Hold the bobble in one hand and use sharp scissors to trim it into a round and even shape.

Embroidery stitches

When embroidering on knitting, take the embroidery needle in and out of the work between the strands that make up the yarn rather than between the knitted stitches themselves; this will help make your embroidery look more even.

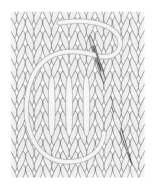

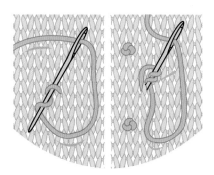

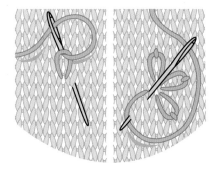

Straight stitch

To make this stitch, simply take the yarn out at the starting point and back down into the work where you want the stitch to end.

French knots

Bring the yarn out at the starting point, where you want the French knot to sit. Wind the yarn around your needle the required number of times, then take it back into the work, just to the side of the starting point. Then bring your needle out at the point for the next French knot or, if you are working the last or a single knot, to the back of your work. Continue pulling your needle through the work and slide the knot off the needle and onto the knitting.

Lazy daisy

Bring the needle and yarn up through the knitted fabric where you want the base of the petal to be, then take it back down through the fabric in the same place, leaving a loop of yarn on the front. Bring the tip of the needle up through the fabric, through the loop of yarn and back down on the other side of the loop to secure it in place. Repeat for each petal.

Swiss darning

Swiss darning (also known as duplicate stitch) is a brilliant technique in which you embroider a new color over the top of one or more stitch(es), as in the Child's pompom hat on page 44. It's also a really useful technique if you've knitted one (or two) of your stitches in the wrong color in a Fair Isle pattern—just Swiss darn the correct color over the incorrect stitch.

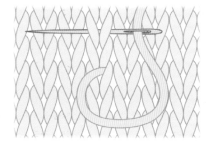

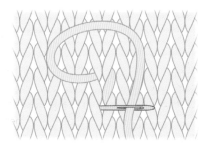

1 Insert a darning/tapestry needle from the wrong side of the work and bring the yarn up in the center of the stitch to be worked on. Take the needle from the right to the left behind both sides of the stitch above the one being worked on, and pull the yarn through.

2 Complete by taking the needle through to the back of the work and tying off the yarn..

Lined knitted pieces

1 Press and block the knitted piece, then measure it. Press the lining to make sure there are no creases. Cut out the fabric lining to fit the knitted piece, allowing an extra 1in. (2.5cm) around each edge for hems. For example, if the knitted piece measures 11 x 8½in. (28 x 21.5cm), cut out a piece of fabric 13 x 10½in. (33 x 26.5cm).

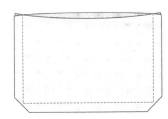

2 Place the two lining pieces with RS together. Pin and sew the side seams, and the bottom seam if there is one, ensuring that the lining is exactly the same measurement, at the sides, as the knitted piece. Trim across the corners. Do not turn RS out.

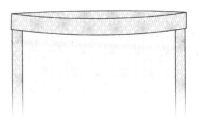

3 Fold the top edge of lining to the outside by 1in. (2.5cm) and press in place.

4 Make up the knitted piece and turn RS out. Insert the lining into the knitted piece, so WS are together. Ease the lining right down inside the knitted piece, so it fits nicely at the bottom. Using long pins, pin the lining to the knitted piece around the opening; start pinning at the side seams, then pin the center (halfway) of each side, then pin in between the center pin and the side seam pin. Add more pins if necessary to ensure it's neatly pinned all round.

5 Using a sewing needle and thread, slip stitch the lining and knitted piece together along the top edge.

6 Add two or three hand stitches in sewing thread on each side of the bottom edges to secure the lining to the knitted piece and keep it in position.

Adding a zipper

The method for this is very similar to the instructions for Lining knitted pieces, with just a few changes to allow for adding a zipper.

1 Press and block the knitted piece, then measure it. Press the lining to make sure there are no creases. Cut out the fabric lining to fit the knitted piece, allowing an extra 1in. (2.5cm) around each edge for hems. For example, if the knitted piece measures 11 x 8½in. (28 x 21.5cm), cut out a piece of fabric 13 x 10½in. (33 x 26.5cm).

2 Place the two lining pieces with RS together. Fold the top edge of lining to the outside by 1in. (2.5cm) and press in place.

3 Pin the WS of the zipper to the WS of the fabric along one of the top hemmed edges and sew in place.

4 Unzip the zipper and sew the other side of the zipper to the opposite side of the fabric.

5 Sew the side edges together. If your zipper is too long for your fabric, sew a stop into the zipper.

6 Make up the knitted piece and turn RS out. Insert the lining into the knitted piece, so WS are together. Ease the lining right down inside the knitted piece, so it fits nicely at the bottom. Using long pins, pin the zipper part of the lining to the knitted piece around the opening; start pinning at the side seams, then pin the center (halfway) of each side, then pin in between the center pin and the side seam pin. Add more pins if necessary to ensure it's neatly pinned all round.

7 Using a sewing needle and thread, slip stitch the zipper/lining and knitted piece together along the top edge.

8 Add two or three hand stitches in sewing thread on each side of the bottom edges to secure the lining to the knitted piece and keep it in position.

suppliers

US STOCKISTS

Knitting Fever
(Debbie Bliss yarns)
Stores nationwide
www.knittingfever.com

The Knitting Garden
(Debbie Bliss yarns)
www.theknittinggarden.org

Webs
(yarn, accessories, tuition)
75 Service Center Rd
Northampton, MA 01060
www.yarn.com
customerservice@yarn.com

Wool2Dye4
(range of British yarns)
www.wool2dye4.com

Accessories
A.C. Moore
(accessories)
Online and east coast stores
www.acmoore.com
1-888-226-6673

Hobby Lobby
(accessories)
Online and stores nationwide
www.hobbylobby.com
1-800-888-0321

Jo-Ann Fabric and Craft Store
(accessories)
Stores nationwide
www.joann.com
1-888-739-4120

Michaels
Stores nationwide
www.michaels.com
1-800-642-4235

UK STOCKISTS

Mrs Moon
(yarns)
www.mrsmoon.co.uk
info@mrsmoon.co.uk

Fyberspates
(yarns)
Unit 3, Prospect Park,
Parkway, Deeside
Chester
CH5 2NS
+44 79546 948378
fyberspates.com

Chester Wool Co
(yarns)
www.chesterwool.com
chesterwool@btinternet.com

Deramores
(yarn, knitting needles, accessories)
0800 488 0708 or 01795 668144
www.deramores.com
customer.service@deramores.com

Designer Yarns
(distributor for Debbie Bliss yarns)
www.designeryarns.uk.com

Love Knitting
(yarn, knitting needles, accessories)
www.loveknitting.com
+44 845 544 2196

Wool Warehouse
(yarn, knitting needles, accessories)
www.woolwarehouse.co.uk
0800 505 3300
sales@woolwarehouse.co.uk

Tuition
Nicki Trench
Craft Clubs, workshops, accessories
www.nickitrench.com
nicki@nickitrench.com

index

acknowledgments

I have very much enjoyed designing and making these rainbow projects, but I couldn't have done it on my own and I feel very lucky to have so many fantastic people in the background helping and supporting me through the whole process.

I would like to say a huge thank you to Cindy Richards for commissioning me, Penny Craig for doing a fabulous job of project managing, and Sally Powell and the rest of the team at CICO Books for putting together such a lovely book. Thank you to the stylist Isabel de Cordova and photographer Caroline Arber for doing such a great job too. And thanks also to Alison Fenton for her stylish design and Stephen Dew for the very clear techniques artworks.

Thank you to Jane Czaja, who is the best pattern-checker I've ever worked with and who is meticulous and very generous with her time at sorting any challenging patterns out. Thanks also to Marie Clayton, who, as always, has made an exceptional job of the editing. I'd also like to say a big thank you to Bronagh Miskelly who sorts out the grading and sizing for all the garments.

Although I make a majority of the projects for the photography myself, I also have a really great team of reliable and expert knitters, without whom I would never be able to reach the deadlines. They are Tina McAra, Bronagh Miskelly, Mel Howes, Anne Hann, and Tracey Elks. Also a big thanks to Vikki Haffenden for bailing me out by letting me use her computer software for the Fair Isle charts, when my computer died and I was unable to use it anymore.

I'm very lucky to have access to some really beautiful yarns and more than that, some really great suppliers. Special thanks to Graeme Knowles-Miller and Rhiannon Evans from Designer Yarns, who are exceptionally quick at getting the yarns out and really helpful when I couldn't find just the right color. It got particularly tricky sorting out so many colors for this book! Thanks also to Jeni Hewlett from Fyberspates for her gorgeous silk yarns and Mrs Moon for their gorgeous "Plump" yarns.